Beautiful, Bountiful
OREGON

A COLLECTOR'S BOOK OF RECIPES AND TRAVEL IDEAS

Photography by
DAN CALLAGHAN

Design by
TIM FAYTINGER

ASSISTANCE LEAGUE® OF CORVALLIS

Assistance League of Corvallis, Oregon, is a nonprofit organization and one of more than 100 chapters and guilds of National Assistance League.® Chartered in 1970, the Corvallis chapter has developed various philanthropic projects to meet needs within Benton County, Oregon. Chapter members devote more than 15,000 volunteer hours each year in service to the community.

Proceeds from the sale of *Beautiful, Bountiful Oregon* will be used to support community projects of Assistance League of Corvallis and will benefit Benton County children.

Library of Congress Catalog Card Number: 96-85715

ISBN: 0-96-16597-1-8

Printed by Graphic Arts Center, Portland, Oregon

To obtain additional copies of *Beautiful, Bountiful Oregon*, please send $27.95 ($23.95 + $4.00 shipping/handling) to: Assistance League of Corvallis, 547 NW Ninth Street, Corvallis, Oregon 97330

Each recipe in this book has been triple-tested in the kitchens of Assistance League members. The nutritional analysis for each recipe was generated through a computer software program. The analysis is thought to be as accurate as possible, given inherent factors which limit preciseness. Analysis may change according to variations in ingredients, size of portions, and cooks' taste preferences (e.g. "salt to taste").

CONTENTS

WELCOME TO BEAUTIFUL, BOUNTIFUL OREGON

*W*hile every state in the country has its beauty and attractions, Oregon seems particularly blessed with an abundance of both. The incredible diversity of settings—giant forests, emerald valleys, spectacular mountains, rushing rivers, golden deserts, crystal-clear lakes, and, of course, the Pacific Ocean—all combine to make Oregon a state of wonders, excitement, and adventure. In addition, the mild climate, fertile soil, and just-right growing conditions make it a highly productive state, leading the nation in the output of many products. In *Beautiful, Bountiful Oregon,* Assistance League of Corvallis is proud to present an overview of the beauty and bounty that make Oregon so attractive.

The Travel section of our book is designed to "whet your appetite" for a visit to our state and its amazingly varied regions. Through beautiful photographs and descriptions of each region, we have spotlighted natural attractions and activities that are enlightening, fun, and well-suited for family outings. Festivals and tourist attractions are included only in cases where they are truly unique or landmarks for the region. We did not attempt to develop a complete tour book of Oregon—the Oregon Tourism Commission and regional tourist agencies already have developed comprehensive publications free for the asking, and we include phone numbers and addresses for them at the end of each region's description.

The Recipes section of *Beautiful, Bountiful Oregon* showcases outstanding recipes from the files of our Assistance League members, families, and friends. Following the wonderful success of our earlier cookbook, *Oregon Sampler: Resorts and Recipes,* we have included all new recipes that are unique, easy to fix, and absolutely delicious. Many of the recipes also feature products that are proudly grown—or raised—in Oregon. In *Beautiful, Bountiful Oregon,* we've also included more recipes that satisfy today's appetite for lighter, lower-fat foods. And to aid in meal-planning for a healthier lifestyle, we feature a nutritional analysis for each recipe.

We offer *Beautiful, Bountiful Oregon* as a lovely travel book to kindle plans for exciting outings…and a hard-working cookbook to inspire tasty family meals and elegant company dinners. Whether your copy of *Beautiful, Bountiful Oregon* finds its way into your living room or onto your kitchen counter, we extend to you our wishes for good food and wonderful times with family and friends.

ASSISTANCE LEAGUE® OF CORVALLIS

Travel

PORTLAND AND THE WILLAMETTE VALLEY

*I*n a state of superlatives, Portland—Oregon's largest city—is one of its brightest jewels. This cosmopolitan city effortlessly combines culture and commerce with serenity and forested beauty. Skyscrapers and Douglas fir trees are equally at home in this exciting metropolis characterized by beautiful architecture, a network of bridges, outstanding restaurants, and more microbreweries than any other city in the nation.

Bordered by the mighty Columbia River on the north and divided east-west by the meandering Willamette River, Portland boasts a picture-perfect skyline with a majestic Mt. Hood rising high above the city to the east. And while Portland is home to several Fortune 500 corporate headquarters, it's also home to Forest Park, the largest forested municipal park in the nation (5,000 acres).

A visit to Portland can include all the glamor offered in any city of size (malls, festivals, galleries, museums, opera, ballet, theatre, etc.). But those looking for a strictly Portland experience will want to visit Washington Park, home of Portland's zoo, the International Rose Test Gardens, and a Japanese garden. Also not to be missed are OMSI (Oregon Museum of Science and Industry), the World Forestry Center, the Portland Art Museum, and the Oregon History Center. Visitors to the "City of Roses" in early June can take in all the fun and fanfare that surround the Portland Rose Festival and its Grand Floral Parade, the second largest all-floral parade in the United States.

Just south of Portland, the lush Willamette Valley emerges and extends past Eugene, embracing the fertile land between the Cascade Mountains and the Coast Range. Here, in what many call "God's Country," rolling farmlands, fruit and nut orchards, and vineyards abound, making this one of the most productive agricultural valleys in the world. Small wonder that the majority of Oregonians have chosen to put down roots in this verdant, highly livable area.

Benevolent year-round temperatures in Portland and the Willamette Valley seldom rise above 85 in the summer or dip below 30 in the winter. When the rare snowfall does occur, it's likely to be greeted with delight (school's out; offices are closed; everyone plays hooky!). Beneficent rainfall occurs mostly between winter and spring, imparting a rich, green luxuriance to the entire valley.

Acres and acres of prolific crops command attention on a drive through this land of plenty. From spring through summer, riotous displays of tulips, iris, and dahlias form a rainbow of colors in fields that stretch as far as the eye can see. And spring through fall, no visit is complete without a stop at one of numerous roadside stands selling samples of fresh-from-the-field foodstuffs and flowers.

Within the Portland and Willamette Valley area are four of the state-owned colleges or universities: Portland State University (Portland); Western Oregon State College (Monmouth); Oregon State University (Corvallis); and University of Oregon (Eugene). Their presence ensures a full range of intellectual pursuits, cultural offerings, and athletic events to their communities.

Jogging, bicycling, and walking are some of the most popular outdoor activities here, so miles of bike paths add convenience for all three sports. Also, picturesque rivers and lakes dot the region, offering recreation either within or just minutes from populated areas.

OREGON

UNIQUE ATTRACTIONS

Covered bridges
Historic districts (Albany, Aurora,
     McMinnville, Newberg, Salem)
Old Town (Portland)
State Capitol (Salem)
End of the Oregon Trail Interpretive
     Center (Oregon City)
The Falls at Oregon City
Powell's Books (Portland), bookstore
     with the largest number of volumes
     in the United States
Portland Rose Festival and Grand Floral
     Parade (June)
Salem Art Fair & Festival (July)
Timber Carnival (Albany, July)
daVinci Days, a celebration of art,
     science, and technology
     (Corvallis, July)
Oregon Bach Festival (Eugene,
     June–July)
Scandinavian Festival (Junction City,
     August)
Oktoberfest (Mt. Angel, September)

FUN THINGS TO DO

Boat, waterski, fish the Willamette River
Hike and view 10 waterfalls at Silver
     Falls State Park
Tour dozens of wineries and
     microbreweries

Hike or mountain bike on trails and
     roads in 7,000-acre McDonald Forest
     (Corvallis)
Boat, waterski, fish at reservoirs (Green
     Peter, Foster, Santiam)
Camp, fish, hike at Fall Creek Reservoir,
     Willamette National Forest, Waldo
     Lake, Detroit Lake, Santiam River
Sail, windsurf, waterski at Fern Ridge
     Reservoir (near Eugene)
Bike or jog along the 100-mile bikeway
     system in Eugene ("jogging capital of
     the world")
Fly-fish or go white-water rafting on the
     McKenzie River
Downhill or cross-country ski or
     snowboard at Willamette Pass or
     Hoodoo Ski Bowl
Experience Saturday Market (Portland or
     Eugene—arts, crafts, food)
Take in the Oregon State Fair (Salem,
     late August/early September)

GLORIOUS BOUNTY

Berries: strawberries, boysenberries,†
     loganberries,† raspberries,†
     blueberries,* blackberries†
Peppermint†
Onions, beans, cabbage
Sugar beet seed
Pumpkins
Wine grapes
Iris,* tulips, dahlias, lily bulbs†
Hops*
Hazelnuts†
Lumber*
Nursery stock*
English holly,† Christmas trees†
Grass seed†

PRINCIPAL CITIES/TOWNS AND POPULATIONS

Portland: 495,090 within city limits;
     1.6 million within the metro area
Eugene: 120,560
Salem: 116,950
Beaverton: 61,085
Springfield: 47,740
Corvallis: 46,260
Hillsboro: 44,045
Albany: 35,020
McMinnville: 20,995

FOR MORE INFORMATION

Portland Oregon Visitors Association
25 S.W. Salmon Street
Portland, OR 97204
1-800-962-3700

Willamette Valley Visitors Association
P.O. Box 965
Albany, OR 97321
1-800-526-2256

Oregon Tourism Commission
775 Summer Street, N.E.
Salem, OR 97310
1-800-547-7842

*Oregon is one of the nation's largest producers
     of this crop.
†Oregon leads the nation in production
     of this crop.

THE OREGON COAST

Ruggedly beautiful, highly accessible, and somewhat unpredictable, Oregon's coast extends some 300 miles and is a photographer's dream as well as a tourist's delight. The northern and central coast share similar characteristics—shore pines twisted by wind into graceful postures, craggy bluffs overlooking wide sandy beaches, dense forests forming a verdant backdrop. But down south, the scenery changes dramatically to reveal a spectacular area of massive sand dunes and freshwater lakes.

Temperatures at the coast remain mild year-round—60s and 70s in summer, 40s and 50s in winter. The coast gets the lion's share of rain in Oregon, but watching storms come in off the ocean is so popular it counteracts most grumblings about Oregon's "mist." The month of September is generally known as the most promising time to catch a day in the 80s. Or, a visit south to Brookings, Oregon's "Banana Belt," can present a warm, sunny day most any time of the year.

Even at the height of summer, a crowded day at the beach is unlikely. Since all 300 miles of Oregon's beaches are public, there's plenty of room to spread out. Besides, the numerous attractions along the entire coastline help to disperse visitors the length of the state.

The northern coast is particularly rich in history. Astoria gained fame as the first American settlement west of the Rockies, and its hillsides of stately Victorian homes attest to its roots. The impressive 125-foot Astoria Column has a pictorial frieze spotlighting events significant to Northwest history. And nearby is Fort Clatsop, a reconstruction of Lewis and Clark's camp during the winter of 1805–06.

Whale-watching is a popular sport along the coast, as is watching the antics of the playful harbor seals and sea lions in the bays. Crabbing, clamming, and fishing offer chances to reap the bounty of the sea while enjoying an invigorating time outdoors.

In Newport, the Oregon Coast Aquarium is recognized as one of the premier aquariums in the country, offering both indoor and outdoor displays plus North America's largest walk-through sea bird aviary. The Aquarium is also home to Keiko, the orca star of "Free Willie" movies. Next door, the Mark O. Hatfield Marine Science Center features hands-on displays of the marine world.

The coast is famous for its production of world-quality cheeses, helped in no small part by the rich milk produced by contented cows, who benefit from the bountiful rain-fed grass in the region. Several cheese factories in Tillamook and Bandon offer tours and samples. Also interesting to view in Bandon are acres of cranberry bogs, producing bounty for Thanksgiving tables across the nation.

OREGON

UNIQUE ATTRACTIONS

Fort Clatsop

Fort Stevens State Park

The Astoria Column

Megler-Astoria Bridge, the longest
continuous truss bridge in existence

Columbia River Maritime Museum
(Astoria)

Haystack Rock at Cannon Beach

Westward end of the Lewis and Clark
expedition at Seaside

Lighthouses all along the coast

Devil's Churn at Cape Perpetua Visitors
Center and Lookout

Depoe Bay, world's smallest navigable
harbor

Oregon Coast Aquarium

Mark O. Hatfield Marine Science Center

Oregon Dunes National Recreation Area

FUN THINGS TO DO

View Victorian homes (Astoria)

Tour a dairy and see how cheese is made
(Tillamook and Bandon)

Visit Necanicum Estuary Park for a
glimpse of marine and
coastal shorebirds

Walk or jog the beach

Explore tidepools along the beach

Fly a kite on more than seven miles of
beach in Lincoln City

Go crabbing and fishing in the bays

Dig for clams

Hunt for seashells or agates
along the beach

Climb the dunes or try your hand at
off-roading on the dunes

Camp in Honeyman State Park or any of
numerous U.S. Forest Service
campgrounds

Explore Old Town in Florence
or Newport

Watch for whales, harbor seals,
and sea lions

Fish for salmon, steelhead, cutthroat
trout on coastal rivers: Siletz, Alsea,
Coquille

Windsurf or boat on freshwater lakes
or rivers

Admire the flower gardens year-round at
Shore Acres State Park (and enjoy
gardens lighted at Christmastime)

Take a self-guided walk along the
Shrader Old-Growth Trail and the
Oregon Coast Trail (near
Gold Beach)

Vacation at one of many outstanding
resorts offering horseback riding,
swimming, golf, fishing

GLORIOUS BOUNTY

Dungeness crabs, clams, salmon,
steelhead, trout

Cheese (Cheddar, jack, brie), milk and
other dairy products

Cranberries

Lumber*

Myrtlewood*

PRINCIPAL CITIES/TOWNS AND POPULATIONS

Coos Bay: 15,450

Astoria: 10,050

Newport: 9,075

Lincoln City: 6,335

Florence: 6,005

Seaside: 5,655

Brookings: 5,100

FOR MORE INFORMATION

Northwest Oregon Tourism Alliance
(Includes North Coast information)
26 S.W. Salmon Street, Box S5
Portland, OR 97204
1-800-962-3700

Central Oregon Coast Association
P.O. Box 2094
Newport, OR 97365
1-800-767-2064

Southern Oregon Visitors Association
(Includes South Coast information)
P.O. Box 1645
Medford, OR 97501
1-800-448-4856

Oregon Tourism Commission
775 Summer Street, N.E.
Salem, OR 97310
1-800-547-7842

*Oregon is one of the nation's largest producers
of this crop.*

THE COLUMBIA GORGE AND MT. HOOD

*A*cross the top section of the state are two of Oregon's most spectacular natural wonders: the Columbia River Gorge and Mt. Hood. When visitors fly into Portland and have only a day or so to sightsee, a scenic drive on "The Loop" (Portland, Columbia Gorge, Mt. Hood, Portland) provides a quick glimpse of some of Oregon's most awesome beauty.

Temperatures in the Gorge and Hood River Valley range in the 70s and 80s in the summer; higher elevations are usually at least 10 degrees cooler. Snowfall in winter is the norm down to 3,000 feet, but it can also descend upon lower elevations when a big winter storm hits.

A drive through the Columbia River Gorge National Scenic Area unfolds breathtaking views of the "Mighty Columbia," carving its wide path through volcanic basalt and carrying barge traffic, fishing boats, and even a sternwheeler. Along the way are dense green forests, picturesque small towns, and beautiful waterfalls, including Multnomah Falls, which drops a spectacular 620 feet and is the most popular attraction in the state.

Wind is almost always a factor in the Gorge, much to the delight of windsurfers, who have made this area the unofficial "sailboarding capital of the world." Near Hood River, sightseers can delight in the panorama of dozens of colorful windsurfing sails skimming across the Columbia. Driving inland, visitors are likely to be awed by the thousands of acres of fruit orchards on the foothills of Mt. Hood, where cherries, pears, and apples grow in abundance.

A defining landmark for the state, Mt. Hood rises 11,235 feet in the sky and offers year-round entertainment for outdoor enthusiasts. In winter, skiers challenge the mountain at three major ski areas: SkiBowl, America's largest night-ski area; Mt. Hood Meadows, offering both Alpine and Nordic skiing; and Timberline, with its unusually long ski season from mid-November to Labor Day.

A not-to-be-missed monument on Mt. Hood is Timberline Lodge, a lasting tribute to the artisans and craftspeople of the depression era. Supported by the Works Progress Administration (WPA), the workers used mostly Oregon materials to construct a massive ski lodge/resort full of beautiful handcarvings, lovely tapestries and oil paintings, and a 92-foot hexagonal lobby fireplace.

In summer and fall, the Mt. Hood area becomes host to scores of hikers, who take advantage of well-developed trails that accommodate both veteran hikers and novices. Camping, canoeing/kayaking, and fishing are also popular, with several beautiful lakes offering soothing escapes for weary city-dwellers. Seasonally, the Columbia River yields hard-fighting salmon to diligent fishermen.

OREGON

Unique Attractions

Breathtaking falls: Multnomah, Bridal
    Veil, Horsetail, Latourell, Wahkeena
Portland Women's Forum State Park and
    Crown Point, postcard settings for
    picture-taking (Columbia Gorge)
Mt. Hood National Forest
Mt. Hood Festival of Jazz
    (Gresham, August)
Timberline Lodge National
    Historic Landmark
Barlow Road, last leg of the Oregon Trail

Fun Things To Do

Windsurf the whitecaps on the
    Columbia River
Downhill or cross-country ski on
    Mt. Hood
Fish, boat, or camp on Lost Lake, Crystal
    Lake, Timothy Lake, Trillium Lake
Drive the Historic Columbia River
    Highway, which passes 77 waterfalls
Fish for salmon or sturgeon on the
    Columbia River
Visit the Tom McCall Wildflower
    Preserve in Mosier
Watch salmon fight their way upstream
    at Bonneville Dam's Visitor Center

Buy fruit and nuts from roadside stands
Hike through forests, along mountain
    streams, up a mountain
Visit a vineyard and taste wine (try the
    region's fruit wines)
Vacation at one of many outstanding
    resorts offering golf, swimming,
    fishing, horseback riding, skiing

Glorious Bounty

Apples,* cherries, pears,* nectarines
Cereal grains
Salmon, sturgeon
Lumber*

Principal Cities/Towns
and Populations

Gresham: 74,625
The Dalles: 11,325
Troutdale: 10,495
Hood River: 4,875
Sandy: 4,520

For More Information

Columbia River Gorge Visitors
    Association
404 W. 2nd Street
The Dalles, OR 97058
1-800-984-6743

Mt. Hood Information Center
P.O. Box 819
65000 E. Highway 26
Welches, OR 97067
1-503-622-3017

Oregon Tourism Commission
775 Summer Street, N.E.
Salem, OR 97310
1-800-547-7842

*Oregon is one of the nation's largest producers
of this crop.*

CENTRAL OREGON

On dreary days, Oregonians in search of sunshine are apt to trek to Central Oregon, which boasts more than 300 sun-filled days and less than12 inches of precipitation a year. With summers of sunny days and cool nights, plus crisp winter days with lots of sunshine and snow, this region has emerged as a nationally recognized, year-round playground for outdoor enthusiasts of all ages.

Here, being outdoors means being surrounded by snow-capped mountains, pine forests, sagebrush-juniper deserts, pristine mountain lakes, rushing rivers, and meadows lush with wildflowers. If it sounds like heaven on earth, that explains why the area's population has mushroomed and continues to grow at a record rate.

The Deschutes National Forest is the heart of this outdoor wonderland, with almost two million acres of public land, 500 miles of streams, 150 lakes, 20 mountains, and six wild and scenic rivers. The Deschutes River is the region's major waterway, offering world-famous steelhead and trout fishing, white-water rafting, camping, canoeing, and kayaking. In its tamer stretch, the Deschutes flows through the area's largest city, Bend, and forms a small pond in Drake Park, where pic-nickers, ducks, and geese share an idyllic setting.

Just 20 minutes away from Bend, Mt. Bachelor commands due attention as one of the premier ski areas in the West, with more than 200 inches of dry powder snow a year. Beyond the mountain on the Cascade Lakes Highway lies a veritable paradise of lakes and reservoirs offering fishing, windsurfing, and canoeing. In the same area, Three Sisters Wilderness Area offers great camping and backpacking, while Crane Prairie Reservoir is a wonderful spot for viewing nest-ing and feeding osprey.

Much of the area in Central Oregon owes its beginnings to long-ago volcanic eruptions of the Cascade Mountains, and many visitors can't resist hiking among the awesome lava flows. Newberry National Volcanic Monument offers inter-esting lava formations and obsidian fields, an outstanding view from Paulina Peak, and top-notch fishing in two premier lakes, Paulina and East.

Central Oregon is better known for its fun activities than its bounty, but the area does produce several vegetable crops. The beef cattle, horses, and sheep from this region may be the most-photographed animals in the state, as many of them dine in grassy fields with a movie-set backdrop of deep blue skies, puffy white clouds, and snow-capped mountains.

OREGON

UNIQUE ATTRACTIONS

Sisters Outdoor Quilt Show (July)

Beautiful falls: Tumalo, Benham, and Cline

Tygh Valley All-Indian Rodeo (May)

Newberry National Volcanic Monument

Kah-Nee-Ta hot springs and Warm Springs Indian Reservation

Lava River Cave and Lava Cast Forest at Sunriver, with remarkable volcanic history

Llama breeding ranches

Crooked River Gorge

The High Desert Museum south of Bend, with in-depth displays of the history and inhabitants of the high desert

FUN THINGS TO DO

Tour The Museum at Warm Springs Indian Reservation, one of the most impressive tribal collections in the nation

Fish, camp, or go white-water rafting on the Deschutes River

Boat, fish, camp, or rent a houseboat at Cove Palisades State Park, where Lake Billy Chinook is formed by the convergence of the Metolius, Deschutes, and Crooked rivers

Dig for thundereggs, agates, and fossils in the area near Cove Palisades State Park

Climb steep walls and spires at internationally famous Smith Rock State Park

Fly-fish the pristine waters of the Metolius River, one of the nation's largest spring-fed rivers

Fish or camp on any number of high-mountain lakes and streams

Hike the Pacific Crest Trail

Schuss or snowboard down the slopes or cross-country ski at Mt. Bachelor

Drive to the top of Lava Butte and then hike through a lava flow from the Lavalands Visitor Center

View the summer skies at Pine Mt. Observatory

Ride the Summit Chair at Mt. Bachelor in summer and enjoy views from Washington to California

Picnic and feed the fish at the Wizard Falls Fish Hatchery (near Camp Sherman)

Vacation at one of many outstanding resorts offering swimming, fishing, horseback riding, golf, bicycling, winter ice skating

GLORIOUS BOUNTY

Beef cattle, sheep, llamas

Potatoes, carrots, garlic, lettuce, onions, radish seed

Peppermint†

PRINCIPAL CITIES/TOWNS AND POPULATIONS

Bend: 29,425

Redmond: 9,650

Prineville: 5,945

Madras: 4,290

Sunriver: 1,100

Sisters: 765

FOR MORE INFORMATION

Central Oregon Visitors Association
63085 N. Highway 97, #104
Bend, OR 97701
1-800-800-8334

Oregon Tourism Commission
775 Summer Street, N.E.
Salem, OR 97310
1-800-547-7842

† Oregon leads the nation in production of this crop.

EASTERN OREGON

*R*ipe with contrasts and extremes, Eastern Oregon is big, bold, beautiful. Here, summer temperatures of 80 to 100 are common, while winter is crisp, cold, often snowy. Spring ushers in moderate weather that welcomes fields of wildflowers and emerging crops. Rainfall is minimal in most locations; indeed, the southernmost section receives less than 10 inches a year.

Striking in its diversity, Eastern Oregon is home to painted deserts, national forests, mountain ranges, huge lakes, wildlife refuges, far-reaching farms and ranches. In Eastern Oregon, where the Oregon Trail pioneers first rolled their wagons into the state and left still-visible wagon ruts, it's easy to step back in time and recall the Oregon of yesteryear. At the National Historic Oregon Trail Interpretive Center near Baker City, visitors can take an in-depth look at pioneer life. And prehistoric times can be explored through ancient fossil beds in the John Day Basin.

Eastern Oregon is also the heart of Oregon's "gold country," with several gold-mining museums documenting the findings. And for recollection of Oregon's Old West, it's hard to beat Pendleton, home of the world-famous Pendleton Round-up, the Round-Up Hall of Fame, Pendleton Underground, and real working cowboys.

The southern part of this region is clearly for the nature lover who likes wide-open spaces. Malheur Wildlife Refuge stretches 30 miles and is a major feeding stop for 250 species of birds. Steens Mountain is an immense 30-mile long, 9,700-foot-high mass that rises majestically off the desert floor. And for the young at heart, Alvord Desert is host to "landsailors," who skim across the dry alkaline mud on wheel-mounted sailboards.

Nature's bounty ranges from the ordinary to the sublime in Eastern Oregon. Orchard fruits include apples, cherries, and plums, while melons from this area are prized throughout the Northwest. Rolling acres of golden wheat and fields of potatoes attest to Eastern Oregon's fertility, while onions take root in Ontario, the "onion capital of the continent."

Eastern Oregon towns abound with museums, galleries, and art colonies, many of which focus on early Oregon or the great outdoors. Also located here is Eastern Oregon State College (La Grande), which offers a wide variety of classes and cultural events.

OREGON

UNIQUE ATTRACTIONS

Pendleton Round-Up (September)
National Historic Oregon Trail
    Interpretive Center (Baker City)
John Day Fossil Beds and the
    Painted Hills
Start of the Oregon Trail in
    Oregon (Nyssa)
Hell's Canyon, the continent's
    deepest gorge
National Antelope Refuge at
    Hart Mountain
Alvord Desert, with sand dunes, playa
    lakes, hot springs, salt desert
    vegetation
Jordan Valley, home of Jordan Craters
    and Pillars of Rome (chalk-
    colored cliffs)
Umatilla National Wildlife Refuge

FUN THINGS TO DO

Go hang-gliding near Lakeview, the
    "Hang-Gliding Capital of
    the Northwest"
Hunt for gemstones in the
    Warner Valley
Boat, camp, hike at Goose Lake,
    Wallowa Lake State Park, and dozens
    of other parks

Fish the Grande Ronde River, Wallowa
    Lake, and myriad lakes and streams
Hunt for thundereggs near Nyssa,
    "Thunderegg Capital of Oregon"
Go white-water rafting on the Snake and
    Owyhee rivers
Hike, camp, fish, horse-pack in Wallowa
    Mountains and Eagle Cap
    Wilderness, the "Switzerland
    of America"
Cross-country ski or snowmobile in the
    Blue Mountains, Ferguson Ridge,
    Mt. Howard
Downhill or cross-country ski at
    Anthony Lakes
Explore the Hells Canyon National
    Recreation Area—215,000 acres
    offering hiking, jet-boat tours,
    fishing, rafting, backpacking, llama
    trekking, horseback riding
Fly-fish the Umatilla River on the
    Umatilla Indian Reservation
Go birding at Malheur National
    Wildlife Refuge
Pan for gold!

GLORIOUS BOUNTY

Wheat, oats, alfalfa, barley
Grass seed†
Cherries, apples,* plums, melons
Onions, potatoes, asparagus, peas,
    garbanzo beans
Peppermint†
Beef cattle, sheep, horses, llamas
Lumber*

PRINCIPAL CITIES/TOWNS AND POPULATIONS

Pendleton: 15,715
La Grande: 12,195
Ontario: 9,760
Baker City: 9,585
Milton-Freewater: 5,865
Burns: 2,870
John Day: 1,900

FOR MORE INFORMATION

Eastern Oregon Visitors Association
P.O. Box 1087
Baker City, OR 97814
1-800-332-1843

Oregon Tourism Commission
775 Summer Street, N.E.
Salem, OR 97310
1-800-547-7842

*Oregon is one of the nation's largest producers
    of this crop.
†Oregon leads the nation in production
    of this crop.

SOUTHERN OREGON

A unique combination of wilderness and culture, Southern Oregon presents a cornucopia of excitement for a wide variety of tastes. Here, it's possible to ride the white water of a scenic wild river in the morning, explore gold-rush towns in the afternoon, then settle back for a Shakespearean play in the evening. And that's only the beginning.

Separated geographically from the state's more populous areas, Southern Oregon is home to two of Oregon's most famous natural wonders, Crater Lake and the Oregon Caves National Monument. Crater Lake (Oregon's only national park) is a striking cobalt blue in color and drops to a depth of almost 2,000 feet, the deepest lake in the United States. The Oregon Caves National Monument, within the Siskiyou Mountains, showcases stalagmites, stalactites, and other formations in room-sized chambers.

The rivers in Southern Oregon are legendary. The North Umpqua, favorite haunt of author Zane Grey, offers world-class steelhead fishing as it works its way seaward. Farther south, the Rogue River, designated "Wild and Scenic," provides steelhead and salmon fishing, jet-boat tours, white-water rafting, and kayaking in a dramatic canyon teeming with wildlife.

Blessed with summertime temperatures in the 80s and 90s and winter temperatures rarely below freezing, the Rogue River Valley boasts huge fruit orchards, most notably pears, peaches, and apples. Wine grapes also flourish here, and numerous wineries dot the countryside. High-desert areas and the Cascade mountains generally have warm summer days and cool nights, plus good snow in the winter. With approximately 250 days of sunshine a year, Southern Oregon is a year-round mecca for visitors.

Culture-seekers can enjoy the Tony Award-winning Oregon Shakespeare Festival (mid-February through October), which draws visitors from around the world to Ashland, the southernmost town along Oregon's Interstate 5 freeway. Nearby is Jacksonville, an early gold-rush town which is one of only eight cities in the U.S. designated a National Historic Landmark. In Jacksonville, amidst antique shops, historic buildings, and museums, the Britt Festival offers a summer-long outdoor music festival that draws top jazz, pop, and classical musicians. Two institutions of higher education—Oregon Institute of Technology (Klamath Falls) and Southern Oregon State College (Ashland)—also offer educational and cultural activities.

UNIQUE ATTRACTIONS

Crater Lake National Park
Railroad Park (Medford)
Pacific Northwest Museum of Natural
    History (Ashland)
Wildlife Safari (Winston)
Oregon's "Redwood Highway" in the
    Illinois Valley
Southern Oregon Historical Society
    Museum (Medford)

FUN THINGS TO DO

Go birding at 20,000-acre Klamath
    Basin, home of seven bird sanctuaries
    with huge numbers of waterfowl and
    migrating waterbirds, plus winter
    habitat for hundreds of eagles and
    hawks
Fly-fish for winter and summer steelhead
    on the North Umpqua, maybe even
    hook a chinook or coho salmon or
    wild brown trout
Take a jet-boat tour up the Rogue River
    and spot black bears, bald eagles,
    blue herons, salmon jumping
Run the Rogue River in a raft or kayak;
    fish for steelhead or salmon; hike
    or camp
Tour wineries and taste Chardonnay,
    Gewurztraminer, Merlot, Cabernet
Go spelunking in Oregon Caves
    National Monument
Try hot-air ballooning in Grants Pass
Tour Oregon's largest fish hatchery at
    Lost Creek Reservoir
Fish, boat, hike at Diamond Lake; cross-
    country ski and snowmobile
    in winter
Visit the nation's largest logging museum
    at Collier State Park
Climb Table Rock outside Medford
Downhill or cross-country ski at
    Mt. Ashland
Camp, hike, fish at Howard Prairie
    Lakes, Winema National Forest,
    Illinois River State Park, Umpqua
    National Forest
Boat or fish Upper Klamath Lake,
    Oregon's largest natural lake

GLORIOUS BOUNTY

Forest products*
Pears,* apples,* peaches
Livestock
Feed barley
Potatoes and field crops
Wine grapes

PRINCIPAL CITIES/TOWNS AND POPULATIONS

Medford: 53,280
Roseburg: 18,910
Grants Pass: 18,830
Klamath Falls: 18,405
Ashland: 17,725
Jacksonville: 2,005

FOR MORE INFORMATION

Southern Oregon Visitors Association
P.O. Box 1645
Medford, OR 97501
1-800-448-4856

Oregon Tourism Commission
775 Summer Street, N.E.
Salem, OR 97310
1-800-547-7842

* Oregon is one of the nation's largest producers of this crop.

Schoolhouse at Summer Lake
(Eastern Oregon)

Portland and Mt. Hood from
Washington Park

Crater Lake (Southern Oregon)

Covered bridge over North Fork of
Yachats River (Coast)

Opposite Page
State Capitol at Salem (Willamette Valley)

Previous Pages
Windsurfers on the Columbia River
(Columbia Gorge)

Columbia River near mouth of
Deschutes River (Columbia Gorge)

Opposite Page
Forest with fall foliage (Southern Oregon)

North Umpqua River (Southern Oregon)

Previous Pages
Painted Hills (Eastern Oregon)

Field of tulips (Willamette Valley)

Opposite Page
Balanced rocks and Lake Billy Chinook
(Central Oregon)

Old barn near Hebo (Coast)

Following Page
Mt. Bachelor ski area, with the
Three Sisters mountains in background
(Central Oregon)

Appetizers

8 ounces cream cheese, softened
½ cup vanilla yogurt
2 tablespoons firmly packed brown
    sugar
½ teaspoon ground ginger
¼ teaspoon ground cinnamon
1 tablespoon freshly squeezed lemon
    juice
1 teaspoon grated lemon peel
¼ teaspoon vanilla extract
½ cup freshly grated apple

Apple, pear, honeydew, or
    cantaloupe slices, for dipping

GINGER-APPLE DIP

Serve this slightly sweet dip with fresh fruit.

Yield: 10 servings

In a medium bowl, blend together the cream cheese and yogurt. Stir in remaining ingredients. Spoon into a serving bowl, cover tightly, and chill until ready to serve.

NOTE

Low-fat or nonfat cream cheese and yogurt can be used successfully in this recipe.

Nutrition Facts Per Serving (dip only): 97 calories, 8 g total fat (5 g saturated), 26 mg cholesterol, 4 g carbohydrate, 2 g protein, 73 mg sodium

24 slices bacon
4 ounces cream cheese
½ cup whole-milk ricotta cheese
½ teaspoon hot pepper sauce
48 large pitted prunes

BACON-WRAPPED PRUNES

This sumptuous bite surprises many, but it is always well-received.

Yield: 24 servings

Preheat oven to 450 degrees. Cook the bacon in a frying pan until limp and partially cooked; set aside to cool.

Blend the cheeses and hot pepper sauce in a food processor until smooth and well mixed. Use a small knife or spoon to stuff the prunes, rounding the cheese on top of the prune. The filling becomes firm as it cooks.

Cut bacon slices in half lengthwise. Wrap a strip of bacon around each stuffed prune. Place prunes on a cookie sheet and bake at 450 degrees for 7 minutes, or until the bacon is crisp. Allow prunes to cool for 5 minutes before serving.

Nutrition Facts Per Serving: 102 calories, 5 g total fat (3 g saturated), 13 mg cholesterol, 11 g carbohydrate, 3 g protein, 120 mg sodium

½ cup drained sun-dried tomatoes
    packed in oil (reserve oil)
6 ounces pitted black olives, drained
1 cup grated Parmesan cheese
4 cloves garlic
1 teaspoon lime juice
Pepper to taste

Baguette or crackers

SUN-DRIED TOMATO TAPANADE

A star performer! Quick and easy, and it can be made ahead.

Yield: 12 servings

Using a blender or food processor, blend all ingredients, except pepper, until finely puréed but not completely smooth. Thin with a little of the tomato oil, if needed. Season to taste with pepper.

Serve with baguette slices or crackers.

Nutrition Facts Per Serving (without bread or crackers): 58 calories, 4 g total fat (2 g saturated), 5 mg cholesterol, 3 g carbohydrate, 3 g protein, 260 mg sodium

HUMMUS WITH PITA TOASTS

The pita toasts are wonderful on their own. Wholesome hummus with a cilantro twist is a tasty bonus.

Yield: 16 servings

Preheat oven to 275 degrees.

In a food processor or blender, purée all hummus ingredients.

Split pita bread into rounds. Brush rough surface with melted butter and sprinkle with grated Parmesan cheese. Cut each round into 6 wedges; place on baking sheet. Bake at 275 degrees for 20 minutes.

Garnish hummus with cilantro and serve with cooled pita toasts.

NOTE
For a lighter version, omit butter and Parmesan from pita toasts.

Nutrition Facts Per Serving: 189 calories, 6 g total fat (3 g saturated), 10 mg cholesterol, 26 g carbohydrate, 9 g protein, 215 mg sodium

HUMMUS
1 can (15.5 ounces) garbanzo beans, drained
1 can (15.5 ounces) Great Northern beans, drained
2 tablespoons freshly squeezed lemon juice
½ bunch cilantro, rinsed and stemmed
2 cloves garlic
2 tablespoons olive oil
¼ teaspoon salt
Cilantro sprigs, for garnish

PITA TOASTS
1 package pita bread
Melted butter
Freshly grated Parmesan cheese

FRESH CORN SALSA

This salsa variation combines sweet and spicy. Ideal for a busy day, since you make it well ahead of time.

Yield: 8 servings

In a medium bowl, whisk together ingredients for Lime Dressing. Blend well.

Briefly cook corn in a small amount of water. Refresh in icy water; drain.

In a medium bowl, combine the corn and remaining ingredients except tortilla chips; toss with Lime Dressing. Chill several hours or overnight. Serve with tortilla chips.

Nutrition Facts Per Serving (without tortilla chips): 143 calories, 6 g total fat (1 g saturated), 0 mg cholesterol, 24 g carbohydrate, 3 g protein, 296 mg sodium

2 cups fresh corn
1 small red onion, diced
1 red or orange bell pepper, diced
5 stalks celery, finely chopped
1 cup chopped fresh cilantro leaves

Tortilla chips

LIME DRESSING
¼ cup freshly squeezed lime juice
3 tablespoons honey, or to taste
3 tablespoons vegetable oil
2 cloves garlic, minced
2 teaspoons ground cumin
1 teaspoon chili powder
1 teaspoon salt

The thunderegg is Oregon's state rock. When the nondescript, rough-looking rocks are cut open and polished, they reveal exquisite, colorful designs reminiscent of a kaleidoscope.

WARM BLUE CHEESE DIP

7 slices bacon, diced
2 cloves garlic, minced
8 ounces cream cheese, room temperature
¼ cup half-and-half cream
4 ounces blue cheese, crumbled
2 tablespoons chopped fresh chives
3 tablespoons chopped smoked hazelnuts

French bread

Oregon hazelnuts are the perfect finishing touch to this zesty combination.

Yield: 10 servings

Preheat oven to 350 degrees.

Cook bacon in a medium frying pan until almost crisp. Drain off the fat; add garlic and cook until bacon is crisp.

Using an electric mixer, beat cream cheese until smooth. Add the cream and beat again. Stir in bacon, blue cheese, and chives. Place in a 2-cup baking dish and cover.

Bake at 350 degrees for 30 minutes, removing cover the last 10 minutes. Sprinkle with smoked hazelnuts.

Serve with sliced French bread.

Nutrition Facts Per Serving (without bread): 292 calories, 17 g total fat (9 g saturated), 39 mg cholesterol, 25 g carbohydrate, 10 g protein, 575 mg sodium

CRANBERRY-STUFFED BRIE IN CRUST

1 sheet frozen puff pastry, thawed
1 round (8 ounces) Brie cheese
½ cup crumbled Gorgonzola cheese
¼ cup whole-berry cranberry sauce
¼ cup chopped walnuts, toasted
1 tablespoon milk

Bread or butter crackers

An elegant surprise for winter entertaining.

Yield: 6 servings

Preheat oven to 350 degrees.

Roll out pastry as package directs.

Slice Brie in half horizontally; set top half aside. Spread Gorgonzola over cut side of bottom half of Brie; set reserved half on top, cut side down.

Spread cranberry sauce on top of Brie; top with chopped walnuts.

Place pastry on top of Brie, sauce, and nuts, and carefully wrap pastry over all with edges coming together underneath. Trim away any excess pastry, reserving scraps, and pinching edges to seal.

Place Brie on a baking sheet with seams down. Decorate top with reserved scraps cut into fancy shapes. Brush with milk.

Bake at 350 degrees for 30 minutes, or until crust is golden brown.

Serve warm with thin bread slices or butter crackers.

Nutrition Facts Per Serving (without bread or crackers): 250 calories, 19 g total fat (9 g saturated), 47 mg cholesterol, 10 g carbohydrate, 11 g protein, 423 mg sodium

UMMER BERRY BRIE

This appetizer can be prepared two days ahead and refrigerated.

Yield: 12 servings

Set aside some blueberries for garnish. Combine remaining berries, apple, dates, pecans, and wine in a medium bowl. Marinate 2 hours or longer.

Cut Brie in half horizontally, forming 2 thin circles. Sandwich the marinated fruit mixture between the 2 layers of cheese. The Brie can be refrigerated for up to 48 hours at this point.

Preheat oven to 350 degrees. Place cheese in ovenproof dish; bake for 20 to 25 minutes, or until cheese begins to melt. Do not overcook. Garnish with reserved berries and serve with sourdough baguette slices or crackers.

Nutrition Facts Per Serving (without bread or crackers): 167 calories, 13 g total fat (7 g saturated), 38 mg cholesterol, 5 g carbohydrate, 8 g protein, 239 mg sodium

½ cup fresh blueberries
1 small Golden Delicious apple, cored and diced
5 dates, pitted and diced
⅓ cup chopped pecans
⅓ cup dry white wine
1 round (16 ounces) Brie cheese

Sourdough baguette or crackers

RI-COLOR PÂTÉ

A lovely make-ahead dish that's worthy of any great party.

Yield: 16 servings

Line a 2-cup bowl with plastic wrap, with ends overlapping the outside of bowl.

In a blender, process Pesto ingredients. Set aside.

Cream the cheeses together and divide in thirds.

Process the tomatoes and garlic in a blender until smooth.

To assemble the pâté, layer in plastic-wrapped bowl: ⅓ cheese mixture, pesto, ⅓ cheese mixture, tomato-garlic mixture, ⅓ cheese mixture. Cover the pâté with the overlapping plastic wrap and refrigerate for 4 hours.

Before serving, prepare Olivada by processing all ingredients in a blender.

At serving time, unmold the pâté and peel off the plastic wrap. Place on a serving plate and top the pâté with the Olivada.

Serve with thin baguette slices or crackers.

NOTE
For convenience, ready-made pesto can be used.

Nutrition Facts Per Serving (without bread or crackers): 125 calories, 10 g total fat (3 g saturated), 13 mg cholesterol, 6 g carbohydrate, 4 g protein, 346 mg sodium

8 ounces low-fat cream cheese
3 ounces feta cheese
¾ cup drained sun-dried tomatoes packed in oil
1 clove garlic

Baguette or crackers

PESTO
2 cloves garlic
1 cup fresh basil
1 cup fresh parsley
¼ cup pine nuts, toasted
3 tablespoons olive oil

OLIVADA
12 ounces pitted Kalamata olives
3 tablespoons olive oil
2 tablespoons pine nuts, toasted
2 large cloves garlic

2 jars (6 ounces each) marinated
    artichoke hearts
1 package (10 ounces) frozen
    chopped spinach, thawed and
    drained
2 cloves garlic, minced
½ cup low-fat sour cream
½ cup low-fat mayonnaise
1 cup grated Parmesan cheese
2 cans refrigerated crescent rolls

 Artichoke-Spinach Rolls

The creamy filling for these quick roll-ups can also be served as a hot dip.

Yield: 16 servings

Preheat oven to 375 degrees. Lightly grease a baking sheet.

Drain and chop the artichoke hearts. In a medium bowl, combine artichokes, spinach, garlic, sour cream, mayonnaise, and grated Parmesan cheese.

Unroll crescent rolls and separate into triangles. Place a heaping teaspoon of the filling on the wide end of each triangle; roll and form a crescent. Place on the prepared baking sheet.

Bake at 375 degrees for 11 to 13 minutes or until lightly browned. Serve at once.

NOTE

To make a hot dip for vegetables, breadsticks, or crackers, place the filling mixture in a casserole and bake at 375 degrees for 20 to 25 minutes.

Nutrition Facts Per Serving: 161 calories, 9 g total fat (3 g saturated), 5 mg cholesterol, 17 g carbohydrate, 6 g protein, 483 mg sodium

¼ cup chopped fresh parsley
2 cloves garlic, minced
¾ teaspoon crushed dried red
    pepper
1 cup grated smoked Gouda cheese
1 cup grated Emmentaler cheese
3 tablespoons pine nuts, toasted
2 cans refrigerated crescent rolls

 Smoky Cheese Pinwheels

Spicy red pepper heats a rich cheese filling. Pine nuts add yet another dimension to this easy appetizer.

Yield: 48 pinwheels

Preheat oven to 400 degrees. Grease 2 baking sheets.

In a medium bowl, combine all ingredients except crescent rolls. Stir to mix well.

Separate refrigerated dough into 8 rectangles. Spread filling over the rectangles, being sure to cover to edges. Roll up jellyroll fashion. Cut each roll into six ½-inch slices; place on the prepared baking sheets.

Bake at 400 degrees for 8 to 10 minutes. Serve hot or cold.

Nutrition Facts Per Pinwheel: 52 calories, 3 g total fat (1 g saturated), 5 mg cholesterol, 5 g carbohydrate, 2 g protein, 119 mg sodium

Cheesy Artichoke Squares

Two cheeses and marinated artichoke hearts flavor this appetizer.

Yield: 36 squares

Preheat oven to 350 degrees. Grease a 9-inch square baking pan.

Drain artichoke hearts; reserve marinade from 1 of the jars. Chop artichoke hearts and set aside.

In a medium frying pan, heat the reserved marinade. Sauté onion and garlic in marinade. Remove from heat; set aside.

In a medium bowl, combine beaten eggs, bread crumbs, and seasonings. Fold in cheeses and reserved artichokes; stir in sautéed onions and garlic.

Pour into prepared pan. Bake at 350 degrees for 30 minutes. Cool slightly before cutting into 1½-inch squares. May be served warm or cold.

Nutrition Facts Per Square: 49 calories, 3 g total fat (1 g saturated), 29 mg cholesterol, 1 g carbohydrate, 3 g protein, 162 mg sodium

2 jars (6 ounces each) marinated
    artichoke hearts
1 small onion, diced
1 clove garlic, minced
4 large eggs, beaten
¼ cup dry unflavored bread crumbs
½ teaspoon salt
⅛ teaspoon pepper
¼ teaspoon dried oregano
1 cup grated Parmesan cheese
1 cup grated Cheddar cheese

Piquant Olive Toasts

A versatile appetizer that's also a great accent to soups or salads.

Yield: 24 servings

Finely chop olives and set aside in a medium bowl.

With food processor or blender running, drop in garlic, Parmesan cheese, butter, and olive oil. Blend to a paste and stir into the chopped olives. Fold in the grated Jack cheese and basil; mix well.

To serve, preheat broiler. Spread olive mixture on bread slices, place on baking sheet, and broil until bubbly and lightly browned.

Nutrition Facts Per Serving (with bread): 78 calories, 5 g total fat (2 g saturated), 7 mg cholesterol, 6 g carbohydrate, 2 g protein, 177 mg sodium

¾ cup Kalamata olives, pitted
½ cup pimiento-stuffed green olives
3 cloves garlic
½ cup freshly grated Parmesan
    cheese
3 tablespoons butter
3 tablespoons virgin olive oil
½ cup grated Monterey Jack cheese
¼ cup chopped fresh basil
1 fresh crusty baguette, thinly sliced

8 ounces fresh crab meat, cooked
1 can (5 ounces) water chestnuts
½ bunch green onions, finely
    chopped
1 ripe avocado, mashed
2 tablespoons low-fat mayonnaise
2 tablespoons low-sodium soy sauce
Lettuce leaves

Crackers

Avocado Crab

A winning combination of textures and colors.

Yield: 6 servings

Pick over crab to remove any shell. Finely mince or grate the water chestnuts.

In a medium bowl, combine all ingredients; chill.

Serve mixture heaped on lettuce leaves accompanied by crackers.

Nutrition Facts Per Serving (without crackers): 115 calories, 6 g total fat (1 g saturated), 36 mg cholesterol, 7 g carbohydrate, 9 g protein, 319 mg sodium

1½ pounds large shrimp, peeled and
    cooked
1 cup freshly squeezed lime juice
1 medium red onion, sliced into
    thin rings
¼ cup virgin olive oil
2 tablespoons white wine
Salt and pepper to taste
8 Kalamata olives
8 stuffed green olives

Seaside Shrimp

This Pacific Northwest favorite is easy to prepare and always a hit.

Yield: 6 servings

In a nonmetallic bowl, toss together shrimp and lime juice. Refrigerate 4 hours, tossing mixture to coat once or twice.

Stir in sliced onion, olive oil, wine, and salt and pepper to taste; refrigerate and marinate 4 more hours.

To serve, drain off liquid, arrange mixture on serving platter, and garnish with olives.

Nutrition Facts Per Serving: 230 calories, 12 g total fat (2 g saturated), 221 mg cholesterol, 7 g carbohydrate, 24 g protein, 358 mg sodium

1 tablespoon vegetable oil
½ pound sea scallops
2½ teaspoons curry powder, divided
1 small onion, chopped
1 red bell pepper, chopped
¼ cup mango chutney, chopped
1 teaspoon soy sauce
1 small tomato, seeded and chopped

Baguette

Curried Scallop Bites

Rich, exotic hors d'oeuvres that are hearty yet elegant.

Yield: 20 servings

Heat oil in a medium frying pan and sauté scallops and ½ teaspoon curry powder until the scallops are opaque. With a slotted spoon, remove the scallops; set aside.

In the same pan, sauté the onion, pepper, and remaining curry until the vegetables are tender, about 10 minutes. Add the chutney and soy sauce. Cook 1 minute.

Return the scallops to the pan, add the tomatoes, and heat through.

Serve mixture on baguette slices.

Nutrition Facts Per Serving (without bread): 24 calories, 1 g total fat (0.1 g saturated), 4 mg cholesterol, 3 g carbohydrate, 2 g protein, 69 mg sodium

MUSHROOM-FILLED SPINACH ROULADE

This light spinach soufflé is filled with creamy mushrooms and rolled before final baking. Slice and serve hot as a first course.

Yield: 16 servings

Line a jellyroll pan with foil and grease the foil. Preheat oven to 275 degrees.

In a medium saucepan, melt butter; stir in flour to blend. Whisk in milk to form a white sauce. Season with salt, pepper, and nutmeg. Remove from heat.

Beat egg yolks until foamy; add a small amount of the white sauce and stir to blend. Add yolk mixture to the remaining white sauce, whisking to blend well.

Squeeze the spinach to remove most of the liquid; purée in a blender. Add to the white sauce.

In a medium bowl, beat egg whites until stiff; fold into the white sauce mixture. Spread the mixture in the prepared pan. Bake at 275 degrees for 15 to 20 minutes, or until the soufflé is set.

Meanwhile, prepare Mushroom Filling. In a medium frying pan, sauté the mushrooms in the butter. Stir in enough sour cream to form a sauce. Remove from heat. Season with salt and pepper to taste and nutmeg.

Remove the soufflé from oven. Set oven temperature at 350 degrees. Sprinkle soufflé with half the grated Parmesan cheese. Spread mushroom filling over the cheese; sprinkle with the grated Swiss cheese.

Roll up the soufflé from the long side; top with remaining Parmesan. Bake at 350 degrees for 15 minutes or until heated through. Slice and serve warm. Garnish with a border of parsley.

Nutrition Facts Per Serving: 124 calories, 10 g total fat (6 g saturated), 62 mg cholesterol, 5 g carbohydrate, 5 g protein, 123 mg sodium

2 tablespoons butter
4 tablespoons flour
1 cup 2 percent milk
¼ teaspoon salt
Dash of pepper
Dash of freshly grated nutmeg
3 large eggs, separated
1 package (10 ounces) frozen
    spinach, thawed
½ cup grated Parmesan cheese,
    divided
½ cup grated Swiss cheese
Parsley, for garnish

MUSHROOM FILLING
3 tablespoons butter
1 pound mushrooms, thinly sliced
1 cup sour cream
Salt and pepper to taste
Dash of freshly grated nutmeg

Oregon grows 99% of the entire U.S. commercial crop of hazelnuts. With its unique texture and flavor, the Oregon hazelnut is prized worldwide by chefs, bakers, food manufacturers, and homemakers.

Mushrooms Gruyère

Fit for royalty…as an appetizer or a side dish.

Yield: 10 servings

2 pounds fresh mushrooms
½ cup chopped fresh parsley
1 tablespoon chopped fresh
    dill weed
Salt and pepper to taste
½ cup butter
1 cup grated Gruyère cheese
Additional freshly chopped parsley,
    for garnish

Preheat oven to 400 degrees.

Wipe mushrooms with a damp cloth. Remove stems and set them aside. Cut mushrooms into quarters; place in an attractive baking dish.

Finely chop the mushroom stems; combine with parsley and fresh dill. Season to taste with salt and pepper.

In a small saucepan, melt butter; add to the chopped mushroom mixture. Spoon over quartered mushrooms.

Bake at 400 degrees for 30 minutes. Remove from oven, sprinkle with grated Gruyère, and bake an additional 15 minutes. Garnish with parsley; serve immediately.

Nutrition Facts Per Serving: 158 calories, 13 g total fat (7 g saturated), 37 mg cholesterol, 6 g carbohydrate, 6 g protein, 147 mg sodium

Tomato-Basil Tart

Garnished with fresh basil sprigs and tomato roses, this savory tart is equally suited for a luncheon entrée.

Yield: 16 servings

Pastry for single-crust 9-inch pie
1½ cups grated mozzarella cheese,
    divided
5 Roma tomatoes
1 cup loosely packed fresh basil
    leaves
4 cloves garlic
1 teaspoon lemon juice
¼ cup sliced green onions
½ cup mayonnaise
⅓ cup grated Parmesan cheese
⅛ teaspoon white pepper

GARNISH
Fresh basil sprigs
8 cherry tomato roses

Preheat oven to 450 degrees. Place rolled-out pastry in a quiche pan and press to fit pan. Prick pastry several times with a fork; bake 8 to 10 minutes or until done.

Lower oven temperature to 375 degrees.

Sprinkle ½ cup mozzarella cheese over crust. Cut tomatoes into wedges; drain on paper towels. Place tomatoes on top of cheese.

Using a blender or food processor, purée basil, garlic, lemon juice, and green onions. Distribute mixture over the tomatoes.

In a small bowl, combine mayonnaise, Parmesan cheese, 1 cup mozzarella, and pepper; spread over top of tart.

Bake tart at 375 degrees for 35 to 40 minutes or until golden brown. Serve in wedges, warm or at room temperature, garnished with sprigs of fresh basil and tomato roses.

NOTE
To make a tomato rose, use a serrated knife to cut the unpeeled flesh of a cherry tomato in a continuous spiral from top to bottom. Wind tomato into a rose shape from the bottom to the top.

Nutrition Facts Per Serving: 153 calories, 12 g total fat (4 g saturated), 15 mg cholesterol, 8 g carbohydrate, 5 g protein, 192 mg sodium

Soups

CORNISH LENTIL SOUP

1 tablespoon olive oil
1 Cornish game hen
6 cups chicken broth
1½ cups dried lentils
2 large tomatoes, peeled and chopped
1 medium onion, chopped
2 cloves garlic, crushed
1 large stalk celery, chopped
1 tablespoon Dijon mustard
1 teaspoon dried basil

A wonderfully filling soup for a winter's eve…and this soup is even better the next day!

Yield: 8 servings

In a large Dutch oven or heavy soup pot, brown the game hen on all sides in olive oil over medium heat. Add the broth, lentils, tomatoes, onion, garlic, and celery. Bring to a boil; cover, reduce heat, and simmer 1 to 1¼ hours until lentils are soft and meat is ready to fall off the bones.

Remove the hen from the soup; when hen is cool enough to handle, discard skin and remove meat from bones. Cut meat into bite-sized pieces.

Return meat to soup, add the mustard and basil; simmer 15 minutes to blend flavors.

Nutrition Facts Per Serving: 377 calories, 14 g total fat (4 g saturated), 64 mg cholesterol, 25 g carbohydrate, 38 g protein, 1,498 mg sodium

BLACK BEAN SOUP WITH CILANTRO-LIME CREAM

4 slices bacon, chopped
1 small onion, chopped
2 tablespoons tomato paste
½ cup hot water
2 cups cooked, drained black beans
2 cups chicken broth
2 cloves garlic, minced
½ teaspoon ground cumin
¼ teaspoon hot pepper sauce
¼ cup chopped fresh cilantro leaves

CILANTRO-LIME CREAM
½ cup sour cream (low-fat sour cream also works)
1 tablespoon chopped fresh cilantro leaves
1½ tablespoons freshly squeezed lime juice
Salt to taste

Flavorful cilantro and sour cream add a cooling touch to this peppy soup.

Yield: 4 servings

In a large saucepan, sauté bacon and onion over medium heat until onions are tender. Drain off all fat.

Add tomato paste, hot water, beans, broth, garlic, cumin, and pepper sauce. Bring to a boil, reduce heat, cover, and simmer 30 minutes.

Meanwhile, prepare Cilantro-Lime Cream by combining all ingredients in a small bowl. Stir and chill until ready to use.

Remove soup from heat; stir in cilantro leaves. In small batches, purée the soup in blender or food processor. Return to the saucepan to keep warm for serving.

To serve, ladle hot soup into bowls and drizzle with Cilantro-Lime Cream.

Nutrition Facts Per Serving: 276 calories, 11 g total fat (5 g saturated), 19 mg cholesterol, 28 g carbohydrate, 17 g protein, 1,182 mg sodium

Black Bean-Clam Chowder

Beans and clams form a new alliance in this tomato-based chowder.

Yield: 10 servings

In a medium frying pan, sauté onion and celery in olive oil until tender.

Peel and cube potatoes. In a small saucepan, simmer potatoes in a small amount of water until tender. Drain.

In a large saucepan, combine onion mixture and potatoes with remaining ingredients. Simmer 20 minutes.

Nutrition Facts Per Serving: 145 calories, 0.9 g total fat (0.1 g saturated), 2 mg cholesterol, 30 g carbohydrate, 6 g protein, 331 mg sodium

1 teaspoon olive oil
1 cup chopped onion
1 cup chopped celery
1½ pounds potatoes
1 can (28 ounces) crushed tomatoes
    in purée
¾ cup tomato juice
2 cups cooked, drained black beans
3 cans (6.5 ounces each) chopped
    clams and juice
¼ teaspoon salt
¼ teaspoon pepper
½ teaspoon Worcestershire sauce
½ teaspoon hot pepper sauce

Market Bean Soup

Use your own choice of dried beans and lentils to personalize this thick, rich soup. Some good bean choices: kidney, cannellini, lima, pinto, navy.

Yield: 12 servings

Wash and drain beans and lentils. Place in a large saucepan. Add water, salt, and the ham hock. Tie Quick Garni herbs in cheesecloth and add to pan. Bring to a boil, reduce heat, cover, and simmer 2½ to 3 hours, or until beans are tender.

Add tomatoes, onions, celery, and garlic. Simmer, uncovered, for 1½ hours, or until soup becomes creamy.

Remove ham hock; pick meat from the bones, cut into bite-sized pieces, and add to the soup.

Add sausage and chicken breast pieces to soup. Cover and simmer 40 minutes, or until meats are done. Season with salt and pepper to taste.

Before serving, remove Quick Garni; stir in chopped parsley and wine.

Nutrition Facts Per Serving: 397 calories, 17 g total fat (6 g saturated), 42 mg cholesterol, 38 g carbohydrate, 24 g protein, 938 mg sodium

3 cups dried beans and lentils
3 quarts water
1 tablespoon salt
1 ham hock
1 can (28 ounces) chopped, peeled
    tomatoes
2 medium onions, chopped
6 stalks celery, chopped
2 cloves garlic, minced
1 pound link sausage, sliced
4 boneless, skinless chicken breast
    halves, cubed
Salt and pepper to taste
½ cup chopped fresh parsley
½ cup red wine

QUICK GARNI
½ teaspoon chopped fresh parsley
½ teaspoon fresh thyme
2 bay leaves

2 cups dry navy beans
8 cups chicken stock
2 large potatoes, peeled and diced
1 large onion, chopped
1 carrot, sliced
2 bay leaves
2 cups diced cooked chicken
Salt and pepper to taste

GARNISH
Chopped fresh parsley
Paprika

*N*AVY BEAN AND CHICKEN SOUP

A nice twist on an old favorite—this one uses healthful chicken instead of ham.

Yield: 12 servings

Sort and wash beans. Soak them overnight in 2 quarts of water; drain.

In a large pot, combine beans, chicken stock, potatoes, onion, carrot, and bay leaves. Bring to a boil, reduce heat, and simmer for 3 hours.

When beans are tender, add chicken; simmer 15 minutes longer to heat chicken and let flavors blend. Remove bay leaves. Season with salt and pepper to taste.

Garnish with chopped parsley and paprika.

NOTE
Quick-soak method for beans: Heat beans in 2 quarts water to boiling; let boil 2 to 3 minutes. Remove from heat; cover and set aside for at least 1 hour, up to 4 hours. Discard soak water.

Nutrition Facts Per Serving: 188 calories, 3 g total fat (1 g saturated), 22 mg cholesterol, 26 g carbohydrate, 15 g protein, 847 mg sodium

2 tablespoons butter
2 medium onions, chopped
1 medium carrot, peeled and sliced
    ⅛-inch thick
3–4 medium potatoes, peeled and
    cut into ½-inch cubes
¾ cup diced green pepper
1 cup clam juice
½ teaspoon dried marjoram
½ teaspoon ground rosemary
2 teaspoons salt, or to taste
Pepper to taste
2–3 pounds firm, boneless fish
    fillets, such as cod, rockfish, or
    snapper, cut into 1-inch pieces
2 cups corn, canned or frozen
1 quart 2 percent milk
3–4 tablespoons instant mashed
    potato flakes

GARNISH
½ cup chopped fresh parsley
Paprika
Butter

*C*AMPER'S FISH CHOWDER

This vegetable-rich chowder seems to taste even better when cooked over an open fire on the beach. It may be our imagination…an Oregon beach is a magical place.

Yield: 12 regular or 6 very hearty servings

In a large soup pot, sauté the onions in butter until transparent; remove onions and set aside.

Add 1-quart water and carrot slices to the pot; simmer until carrots begin to soften. Add the potatoes and green pepper; simmer, stirring often, for 15 to 20 minutes. Drain most of the liquid from the vegetables.

Return the onions to the pot and add the clam juice, seasonings, fish, corn, and milk. By the time the soup returns to a simmer, in 20 to 30 minutes, the fish and vegetables will be cooked.

Thicken chowder to desired consistency with mashed potato flakes, allowing time for potato flakes to absorb their full amount of liquid before adding more. Garnish each serving with parsley, paprika, and a pat of butter.

Nutrition Facts Per Regular Serving: 299 calories, 6 g total fat (2 g saturated), 55 mg cholesterol, 34 g carbohydrate, 27 g protein, 566 mg sodium

RAINY-DAY CLAM CHOWDER

Comfort food, Oregon-style. So rich—savor it like dessert.

Yield: 6 servings

Drain juice from clams. Set clams aside and place juice in a large saucepan along with chopped vegetables. Add enough water to cover. Simmer 20 minutes, or until vegetables are tender.

In a small saucepan, melt butter over medium heat. Stir in flour, then cream; cook until smooth and thick, stirring constantly. Add to vegetable mixture, stir to blend, and simmer 15 minutes. Stir in clams and salt and pepper to taste; heat 1 to 2 minutes. Garnish each serving with a pat of butter and chopped parsley.

Nutrition Facts Per Serving: 497 calories, 42 g total fat (26 g saturated), 123 mg cholesterol, 25 g carbohydrate, 8 g protein, 547 mg sodium

2 cans (6.5 ounces each) minced
    clams with juice
1 cup chopped onions
1 cup diced celery
2 cups diced potatoes
¾ cup butter
¾ cup flour
1 quart half-and-half cream
Salt and pepper to taste

GARNISH
Butter
Chopped fresh parsley

OREGON SEAFOOD STEW

Sweet, flavorful Dungeness crab is especially good in this recipe, but any crab will work.

Yield: 10 servings

In a large soup pot, sauté onion, garlic, and fennel bulb in olive oil until tender but not browned.

Stir in tomatoes, tomato sauce, wine, and seasonings. Simmer 30 minutes to allow flavors to blend.

Cut fish into 1-inch pieces; scrub clams. Add fish and scallops to the tomato mixture; simmer 10 minutes. Add clams and cook until shells open. Discard any clams that don't open after cooking. Add shrimp and crab. Heat through, remove bay leaf, and serve immediately.

NOTE
Any combination of seafood may be used.

Nutrition Facts Per Serving: 196 calories, 4 g total fat (0.6 g saturated), 82 mg cholesterol, 8 g carbohydrate, 29 g protein, 545 mg sodium

2 tablespoons olive oil
1 cup chopped onion
2 cloves garlic, minced
½ cup chopped fresh fennel bulb,
    optional
1 can (28 ounces) chopped, peeled
    tomatoes
1 cup tomato sauce
½ cup dry white wine
1 teaspoon dried basil
½ teaspoon dried thyme
½ teaspoon dried oregano
¼ cup chopped fresh parsley
1 bay leaf
½ teaspoon fennel seed
¼ teaspoon pepper
1½ pounds fresh fish, such as perch,
    snapper, or halibut
1 pound fresh scallops
1 dozen fresh steamer clams in shells
1 cup cooked Oregon bay shrimp or
    other small salad shrimp
1 cup Dungeness crab meat

¼ cup olive oil
½ cup diced onions
2 cloves garlic, crushed
1 can (28 ounces) chopped, peeled
    tomatoes
3 tablespoons tomato paste
1 tablespoon chopped fresh basil
1 teaspoon chopped fresh thyme
1 teaspoon chopped fresh tarragon
1 cup chicken broth
2½ cups half-and-half cream
¼ cup brandy
⅓ pound bay scallops
⅓ pound cooked salad shrimp
⅓ pound Dungeness crab meat
Salt and pepper to taste
Thin lemon slices, for garnish

2 tablespoons vegetable oil
1 pound beef round steak or chuck
    roast, cubed
2 cloves garlic, chopped
2 large onions, chopped
8 cups beef stock
½ cup pearl barley
1½ teaspoons paprika
⅛ teaspoon dried marjoram leaves
¼ teaspoon caraway seed
3 medium carrots, sliced
3 medium celery stalks, sliced
3 medium potatoes, chopped
1 can (14.5 ounces) chopped,
    peeled tomatoes
1 can (4 ounces) mushrooms with
    liquid
10 ounces frozen peas, thawed

Tomato-Seafood Bisque

A dash of brandy for flavor, three kinds of shellfish for pizazz.

Yield: 6 servings

In a large saucepan, sauté onions and garlic in olive oil over medium heat until transparent. Add tomatoes, tomato paste, and herbs. Stir and simmer 15 minutes.

Using a food processor or blender, purée the tomato mixture until smooth. Return to pan. Stir in broth, cream, and brandy. Simmer 15 minutes longer.

Add scallops and simmer over medium heat until they are opaque. Add shrimp and crab meat and heat through, being careful not to overcook. Season to taste with salt and pepper.

Garnish each serving with a thin lemon slice.

Nutrition Facts Per Serving: 354 calories, 22 g total fat (9 g saturated), 110 mg cholesterol, 14 g carbohydrate, 21 g protein, 744 mg sodium

Beef-Barley Soup

Peas added at the last minute bring a touch of spring to a hearty winter soup.

Yield: 8 servings

Heat oil in a Dutch oven or stockpot. Add beef, garlic, and onions, stirring frequently until beef is browned. Add beef stock, barley, paprika, marjoram, and caraway seed. Cover and simmer for 1 hour.

Add carrots, celery, potatoes, tomatoes, and mushrooms. Simmer for 30 minutes.

Add peas about 5 minutes before soup is done. Heat through.

Nutrition Facts Per Serving: 297 calories, 13 g total fat (4 g saturated), 33 mg cholesterol, 31 g carbohydrate, 15 g protein, 1,534 mg sodium

Crabbing for Dungeness crab is a favorite activity on the Oregon coast. While many are caught, few are chosen. Only male crabs with a minimum shell width of 5¾ inches can be kept.

CARROT-POTATO SOUP

Lovely to look at, even lovelier to taste.

Yield: 4 servings

In a large saucepan, melt butter over medium heat. Add onion and sauté 5 minutes. Add potatoes and chicken stock; simmer until potatoes are tender. Reserve 1 cup cooked potato cubes.

In a small saucepan, cook carrots in small amount of water until tender yet crisp. Reserve ⅓ cup cooked carrots.

Place remaining potatoes, carrots, and cooking liquids in blender or food processor. Process until smooth. Return to saucepan; add reserved vegetables and dill weed. Season to taste. Thin with additional stock or water to desired consistency, if necessary.

Serve hot, garnished with a sprinkle of dill weed.

Nutrition Facts Per Serving: 188 calories, 4 g total fat (2 g saturated), 8 mg cholesterol, 32 g carbohydrate, 7 g protein, 690 mg sodium

1 tablespoon butter
1 cup chopped onion
1¼ pounds (4 medium) potatoes, peeled and cubed
2½ cups chicken stock
1½ cups peeled and sliced carrots
1 teaspoon dried dill weed, plus some for garnish
Salt and pepper to taste

CREAM OF SPINACH SOUP

The unusual addition of eggs makes this soup particularly rich and satisfying.

Yield: 4 servings

In a medium bowl, whisk together the eggs, melted butter, and flour.

In a large saucepan, combine the remaining ingredients. Add egg mixture; whisk to blend. Bring to a boil over medium-high heat, stirring constantly to avoid scorching.

Serve hot or chilled, garnished with a dollop of sour cream, bacon bits, and a dash of pepper.

Nutrition Facts Per Serving: 262 calories, 16 g total fat (9 g saturated), 144 mg cholesterol, 20 g carbohydrate, 11 g protein, 794 mg sodium

2 large eggs, lightly beaten
2 tablespoons butter, melted
2 tablespoons flour
10 ounces frozen chopped spinach, thawed and drained
1 can (10.5 ounces) condensed cream of potato soup
1½ cups milk
¼ cup sour cream
1 green onion, sliced
1 teaspoon lemon juice
¼ teaspoon dried thyme

GARNISH
Sour cream
Bacon bits
Pepper

Hazelnut-Mushroom Bisque

1½ cups hazelnuts
1 pint half-and-half cream
1 quart 2 percent milk
1½ pounds mushrooms, chopped
8 cloves garlic, minced
3 shallots, minced
3¾ cups chicken stock
1¼ cups medium-dry sherry
Salt and pepper to taste
Chopped fresh chives or parsley, for
    garnish

Elegantly flavored and garnished with hazelnuts, this creamy bisque is all dressed up for a dinner party.

Yield: 10 servings

Preheat oven to 350 degrees. Toast hazelnuts by spreading them on a jellyroll pan and baking for 10 to 15 minutes or until browned. Let cool; turn nuts out onto a kitchen towel and rub to remove the skins. Chop nuts fine; reserve ¼ cup for garnish.

In a large stockpot, mix half-and-half cream, milk, chopped mushrooms, garlic, and shallots. Add chopped hazelnuts, except those reserved for garnish.

Cook soup over medium-high heat for about 1 hour, stirring frequently, to reduce the soup by half. Remove from heat and cool; purée in a blender or food processor.

In a separate pot, boil the chicken stock and sherry until reduced by half, approximately 20 minutes.

Combine the cream mixture and chicken stock mixture in a large pot; reheat. Season with salt and pepper to taste. Serve garnished with the reserved chopped nuts and chopped chives or parsley.

Nutrition Facts Per Serving: 301 calories, 20 g total fat (6 g saturated), 25 mg cholesterol, 17 g carbohydrate, 10 g protein, 366 mg sodium

Eggplant Minestrone

3 tablespoons butter
1 cup chopped onion
2 large cloves garlic, minced
1 medium eggplant, peeled and
    diced
2 small zucchini, thinly sliced
1 can (28 ounces) chopped, peeled
    tomatoes
1 can (16 ounces) kidney beans,
    drained
1 cup dry small-shell macaroni
2–3 drops hot pepper sauce
2–3 cups chicken stock

GARNISH
½ cup chopped fresh parsley
1 cup shredded Swiss cheese

A tasty cheese-parsley garnish melts into this thick vegetable soup.

Yield: 6 servings

In a large saucepan, sauté onion in butter. Add garlic and cook until tender. Add the eggplant and sauté 5 minutes.

Add remaining ingredients, except garnish, and simmer 30 minutes.

To serve, combine parsley with shredded cheese and generously top each serving.

Nutrition Facts Per Serving: 331 calories, 13 g total fat (7 g saturated), 33 mg cholesterol, 39 g carbohydrate, 17 g protein, 1,085 mg sodium

ROASTED PEPPER SOUP

Dramatic red color and fantastic flavor—a "must-try" recipe.

Yield: 8 servings

Preheat broiler.

Slice peppers in half, core, and remove seeds. Lay peppers skin side up on broiler pan; place 4 inches from heat and broil until skins are black. Place peppers in a paper bag, close bag, and let rest 5 minutes. Remove charred skins with a knife and discard; chop the peppers and set aside.

In a large Dutch oven, sauté onion, garlic, and celery in olive oil over low heat until transparent. Add reserved peppers, tomatoes, and broth. Bring to a boil, reduce heat, and simmer 15 minutes. Add cream, if used. Season to taste with Worcestershire sauce, salt, and pepper.

Purée mixture in blender or food processor until smooth. Ladle into bowls, garnish with sour cream and herbs, and serve immediately.

Nutrition Facts Per Serving (without cream): 126 calories, 6 g total fat (3 g saturated), 8 mg cholesterol, 11 g carbohydrate, 8 g protein, 879 mg sodium

3 red bell peppers
2 yellow bell peppers
2 Anaheim peppers
1 jalapeño pepper
1 tablespoon olive oil
1 medium onion, chopped
2 cloves garlic, minced
2–3 stalks celery, chopped
2 large tomatoes, peeled and
    chopped
4 cups chicken broth
1 cup half-and-half cream, optional
¼ teaspoon Worcestershire sauce
Salt and pepper to taste

GARNISH
½ cup sour cream
Fresh basil or parsley leaves

ZESTY CHICKEN SOUP

A chicken-vegetable soup with a south-of-the-border influence—green chilies, cilantro, and fresh lime juice are the definitive flavors.

Yield: 8 servings

In a 6-quart Dutch oven, combine onion, garlic, and chicken stock. Bring to a boil, reduce heat, and simmer 10 minutes.

Add remaining ingredients, except garnish, seasoning with salt and pepper to taste. Cover and simmer 30 minutes.

To serve, ladle soup into serving bowls and top generously with cheese, corn chips, and cilantro sprigs.

Nutrition Facts Per Serving: 341 calories, 17 g total fat (5 g saturated), 42 mg cholesterol, 27 g carbohydrate, 22 g protein, 1,103 mg sodium

1 medium onion, finely chopped
3 cloves garlic, minced
6 cups chicken stock
1 can (28 ounces) chopped, peeled
    tomatoes
1 can (4 ounces) chopped green
    chilies
3 tablespoons chopped fresh
    cilantro leaves
1 teaspoon ground cumin
1 teaspoon sugar
Juice of 2 limes
2 cups chopped cooked chicken
Salt and pepper to taste

GARNISH
1 cup shredded Monterey Jack
    cheese
1 cup broken corn chips
Small cilantro sprigs

2 tablespoons olive oil
2 medium zucchini, shredded
1 medium onion, finely chopped
8 cups chicken broth
2 large eggs, beaten
⅓ cup orzo pasta, cooked as
    package directs
1 tablespoon chopped fresh parsley
Salt and pepper to taste

GARNISH
¼ cup freshly grated Parmesan
    cheese
Freshly ground pepper
¼ cup chopped fresh parsley

Italian Zucchini Soup

Similar to "egg drop" soup or the Italian Stracciatella.

Yield: 6 servings

In a medium frying pan, sauté zucchini and onion in oil. Set aside.

In a large saucepan, bring broth to a boil. Dribble beaten eggs into the broth; do not stir. Add sautéed vegetables, cooked orzo, and 1 tablespoon chopped parsley. Season to taste; heat through.

To serve, ladle soup into bowls and top with grated Parmesan, a grind of fresh pepper, and chopped parsley.

Nutrition Facts Per Serving: 142 calories, 8 g total fat (2 g saturated), 74 mg cholesterol, 7 g carbohydrate, 9 g protein, 815 mg sodium

3 large potatoes, peeled and cubed
½ cup sour cream
1 tablespoon olive oil
1 medium onion, sliced
1 clove garlic, minced
2 tablespoons chopped fresh parsley
½ cup sliced mushrooms
½ cup grated carrot
10 cups water
1 cup beef stock
2 tablespoons freshly squeezed
    lemon juice
¼ cup evaporated skim milk
1 small chili pepper, minced
1 cup diced carrot
¾ cup diced celery
¼ cup sliced green onion
1 can (14.5 ounces) chopped,
    peeled tomatoes
4 cups finely shredded cabbage
½ teaspoon dill weed
Salt and pepper to taste
Additional sour cream, for garnish

Winter Vegetable Soup

Thickened with mashed potatoes and sour cream, this soup boasts all kinds of vegetables!

Yield: 15 servings

In a medium saucepan, boil potatoes in water to cover. Drain and mash with ½ cup sour cream; set aside.

In a large frying pan, sauté the onion in olive oil until transparent; add garlic, parsley, mushrooms, and grated carrot. Reduce heat to low and cook 10 minutes; set aside.

In an 8-quart stockpot, combine water, beef stock, lemon juice, evaporated milk, remaining vegetables (chili pepper through cabbage), and seasonings. Stir in mashed potatoes and sautéed vegetables. Bring to a boil, reduce heat, and simmer 1 hour.

Adjust seasonings and serve with additional sour cream.

NOTE
For a vegetarian soup, use vegetable broth.

Nutrition Facts Per Serving: 70 calories, 3 g total fat (1 g saturated), 4 mg cholesterol, 10 g carbohydrate, 2 g protein, 190 mg sodium

Chili-Corn Chowder

Good any time of year! Warm, spicy, and satisfying—like chili, yet so chock-full of veggies you won't miss the meat.

Yield: 6 servings

In a large pot (at least 6-quart), cook garlic in oil until lightly browned. Add onion, celery, carrot, peppers, and salt; sauté 12 minutes over medium heat, stirring often.

Add the next 10 ingredients (green onion through hot pepper sauce) and cook until carrots are tender, about 10 minutes, stirring often.

Reduce heat to medium-low and continue to cook 5 minutes to develop the flavors, adding a bit more oil if necessary.

Stir in the tomato sauce, crushed tomatoes, water, and tomato paste. Bring to a boil over high heat, stirring often to prevent scorching.

Reduce heat and simmer 30 minutes, stirring occasionally; add water if necessary. Taste and adjust seasonings.

Garnish with thinly sliced green onions or sprigs of fresh parsley and/or cilantro.

Nutrition Facts Per Serving: 267 calories, 11 g total fat (1 g saturated), 0 mg cholesterol, 43 g carbohydrate, 7 g protein, 748 mg sodium

4 tablespoons vegetable oil
2 cloves garlic, minced
1 medium onion, chopped
1 stalk celery, sliced
1 carrot, chopped
1 green bell pepper, seeded and
  chopped
1 red bell pepper, seeded and
  chopped
1 jalapeño pepper, seeded and
  minced
½ teaspoon salt
¼ cup thinly sliced green onion
¼ cup chopped fresh parsley
¼ cup chopped fresh cilantro leaves
2 cups fresh or frozen corn
2 teaspoons chili powder
2 teaspoons ground cumin
½ teaspoon pepper
½ teaspoon dried oregano
¼ teaspoon cayenne pepper
Dash of hot pepper sauce
1 can (15 ounces) tomato sauce
1 can (15 ounces) crushed, peeled
  tomatoes in purée
2 cups water
2 tablespoons tomato paste

GARNISH
Green onions
Parsley sprigs
Cilantro sprigs

The city of Klamath Falls sits atop one of the world's richest stores of geothermal energy. This energy was used by the Klamath Indians for cooking more than a century ago.

12 cups chicken broth, divided
6 boneless, skinless chicken breast
   halves
¼ cup pearl barley
1 can (14.5 ounces) chopped,
   peeled tomatoes
¼ cup catsup
2 large onions, chopped
3 large stalks celery, chopped
3 large carrots, sliced
2 cloves garlic, minced
2 tablespoons chopped fresh parsley
2 bay leaves
1 teaspoon dried oregano leaves
½ teaspoon dried basil leaves
¼ teaspoon pepper
1 cup broken linguini
1 cup cut fresh green beans
1 cup fresh corn

Summer Garden Chicken Soup

Fabulous fresh, but it also freezes well.

Yield: 10 servings

Boil chicken breasts in 6 cups chicken broth for 20 minutes, or until chicken is done. Remove chicken; set aside and cool.

Strain broth into another large stockpot; add 6 more cups of chicken broth. Add next 12 ingredients (barley through pepper). Bring to a boil and simmer for 30 minutes.

Turn up heat to medium-high; add linguini and boil gently for 10 minutes.

Add beans and corn; simmer 5 minutes.

Cut chicken into bite-sized pieces and add to soup. Gently simmer soup until chicken is heated through. Remove bay leaves before serving.

NOTE
A 10-ounce package of frozen mixed vegetables may be substituted for the green beans and corn.

Nutrition Facts Per Serving: 307 calories, 5 g total fat (1 g saturated), 34 mg cholesterol, 35 g carbohydrate, 30 g protein, 2,084 mg sodium

2 cups water
2 cups potatoes, diced
½ cup chopped carrot
½ cup chopped celery
¼ cup chopped onion
1½ teaspoons salt
¼ teaspoon pepper
⅛ teaspoon chili powder
¼ cup butter
¼ cup all-purpose flour
2 cups milk
1 cup Cheddar cheese, shredded
1 can (15.5 ounces) creamed corn

Western Corn Chowder

An irresistible flavor combination.

Yield: 6 servings

Bring water to a boil in a 3-quart pot. Add potatoes, carrot, celery, onion, salt, pepper, and chili powder. Return to boiling and simmer for 10 minutes. Do not drain.

Meanwhile, prepare cream sauce. In medium saucepan, melt butter over low heat. Blend in flour and cook over heat, stirring until smooth and bubbly. Stir in milk; bring to a boil, stirring constantly. Boil 1 minute and remove from heat. Add cheese; stir until melted.

Combine vegetables and cream sauce. Add creamed corn; stir. Reheat, if necessary. Do not boil.

Nutrition Facts Per Serving: 293 calories, 17 g total fat (10 g saturated), 51 mg cholesterol, 28 g carbohydrate, 10 g protein, 992 mg sodium

Salads

MELON MEDLEY WITH CITRUS DRESSING

An ever-so-easy fruit salad with a dressing you will make again and again.

Yield: 8 servings

1 ripe cantaloupe
1 ripe honeydew melon
1½ pounds seedless grapes

CITRUS DRESSING
1 large egg
1 cup sugar
Juice of 1 large orange
Juice of 1 large lemon
1½ teaspoons grated orange peel
1½ teaspoons grated lemon peel

Prepare Citrus Dressing in a small saucepan by combining the egg and sugar, beating with a spoon to mix well. Add the juice and grated peel from the orange and lemon; cook over medium heat until sugar dissolves and mixture thickens. Stir constantly to prevent scorching.

Remove pan from heat and chill dressing.

Peel, seed, and quarter the melons. Cut melon sections lengthwise into ¼-inch slices. Stem the grapes.

Divide melon slices among plates. Arrange alternating melons in a fan formation. Place grapes at point of each fan.

Drizzle dressing over fruit and serve.

VARIATION
Fresh pineapple slices and in-season berries add a festive and delicious change.

Nutrition Facts Per Serving: 215 calories, 1 g total fat (0.2 g saturated), 27 mg cholesterol, 54 g carbohydrate, 3 g protein, 33 mg sodium

HARVEST FRUIT SALAD

Dressed lettuces and fruits are brought to the table and drizzled with a second dressing.

Yield: 6 servings

4 cups leaf lettuces, torn
2 unpeeled pears, cored and sliced
2 ripe persimmons, peeled, cored, and sliced
2 kiwi fruits, peeled and sliced
2 oranges, peeled and thinly sliced in rounds

RASPBERRY-ONION DRESSING
2 tablespoons olive oil
1 tablespoon finely diced red onion
½ cup raspberry vinegar
Salt and pepper to taste

ORANGE-HONEY DRESSING
2 tablespoons honey
2 tablespoons orange juice

Prepare the Raspberry-Onion Dressing by combining ingredients and whisking them in a large salad bowl. In a small bowl, mix the Orange-Honey Dressing.

Add the lettuces to the Raspberry-Onion Dressing and toss to coat.

Arrange prepared fruits on top of the lettuce and drizzle with the Orange-Honey Dressing. Serve immediately.

Nutrition Facts Per Serving: 162 calories, 5 g total fat (0 g saturated), 0 mg cholesterol, 32 g carbohydrate, 3 g protein, 22 mg sodium

Cucumbers with Mint Dressing

Cool mint-flavored cucumbers are a fresh accompaniment to a barbecue.

Yield: 10 servings

Slice cucumbers in half lengthwise. Remove seeds and cut crosswise into ¼-inch slices.

Combine all the dressing ingredients and whisk together.

Marinate the slices in Mint Dressing at least 4 hours. Drain before serving.

NOTE
To make mint vinegar, see "Medley of Flavored Vinegars" on page 138 in the Gifts section.

Nutrition Facts Per Serving: 140 calories, 6 g total fat (0.5 g saturated), 0 mg cholesterol, 11 g carbohydrate, 1 g protein, 11 mg sodium

3 cucumbers, peeled

MINT DRESSING
½ cup chopped fresh mint leaves
¼ cup chopped fresh parsley
2 tablespoons grated orange peel
½ cup olive oil
1 cup mint vinegar
3 tablespoons honey

Three-Tomato Salad

Tomatillos are the third tomato in this marinated salad.

Yield: 8 servings

In a medium frying pan, sauté onion and garlic in oil for 5 minutes. Stir in the wine and tomatillos. Remove from heat.

Combine the onion mixture with the remaining ingredients, except lettuce leaves. Marinate at room temperature for 20 minutes.

Drain tomato mixture and serve in a bowl lined with lettuce leaves.

Nutrition Facts Per Serving: 97 calories, 3 g total fat (0.5 g saturated), 0 mg cholesterol, 10 g carbohydrate, 2 g protein, 12 mg sodium

3 tablespoons olive oil
1 small red onion, diced
1 clove garlic, minced
⅓ cup dry white wine
8 tomatillos, husked, cored, and
     diced
4 tomatoes, seeded and diced
1 pint yellow cherry tomatoes,
     seeded and halved, or 1 large
     yellow pepper, seeded and sliced
Salt and pepper to taste
6 sprigs basil, minced
Lettuce leaves for lining serving
     bowl

2 small potatoes, peeled and cooked
1 jar (6 ounces) marinated artichoke
    hearts, drained
1 head curly endive, sliced
1 medium celery heart, sliced
1 small fennel bulb, sliced
1 teaspoon chopped fresh parsley
1 teaspoon drained capers

DRESSING
1 tablespoon nonfat mayonnaise
1 tablespoon wine vinegar
⅓ cup olive oil
Salt and pepper to taste

Exotic Endive Salad

Refreshingly different to both the eye and the palate.

Yield: 6 servings

To prepare dressing, gradually add wine vinegar and olive oil to mayonnaise in a small bowl; season to taste.

Slice potatoes; quarter artichoke hearts. Combine potatoes and artichokes with remaining salad ingredients in a large bowl. Pour dressing over salad, tossing carefully until ingredients are well-coated.

Nutrition Facts Per Serving: 201 calories, 15 g total fat (2 g saturated), 0 mg cholesterol, 17 g carbohydrate, 3 g protein, 185 mg sodium

1 head red leaf lettuce, roughly torn
½ bulb fresh fennel, julienned
18 asparagus spears, blanched and
    cut into bite-sized pieces
3 tablespoons pine nuts, toasted

SESAME DRESSING
1 teaspoon Dijon mustard
½ teaspoon sugar
2 tablespoons red wine vinegar
2 tablespoons sesame seeds, toasted
1 tablespoon Worcestershire sauce
2 cloves garlic, minced
Salt to taste
Freshly ground pepper to taste
2 tablespoons olive oil
2 tablespoons vegetable oil
1 tablespoon minced fresh fennel
    herb

Asparagus-Fennel Salad

Unusual, tangy dressing, plus a sprinkle of pine nuts for crunch.

Yield: 8 servings

Put dressing ingredients in a lidded jar and shake until thoroughly mixed. Refrigerate until ready to use.

In a large bowl, mix red leaf lettuce and fennel; add half of the dressing, tossing well. Arrange greens on salad plates; place asparagus in the center of each. Drizzle additional dressing over the asparagus and top with pine nuts.

Nutrition Facts Per Serving: 109 calories, 10 g total fat (1 g saturated), 0 mg cholesterol, 4 g carbohydrate, 2 g protein, 47 mg sodium

With 12 different varieties of hops grown in the Willamette Valley, it's no surprise that Oregon has more brewpubs and breweries per capita than anywhere in the U.S.

Oregon Hazelnut Salad

Try this combination of sweet and savory flavors in a very appealing green salad.

Yield: 6 servings

In a small bowl, prepare the dressing by whisking together the vinegar and sugar until the sugar dissolves.

Slice the tomatoes into strips. In a large salad bowl, combine greens, tomatoes, currants, and hazelnuts. Toss to mix. Top with the crumbled blue cheese.

At the table, toss salad with the dressing and serve.

Nutrition Facts Per Serving: 135 calories, 5 g total fat (1 g saturated), 4 mg cholesterol, 22 g carbohydrate, 3 g protein, 132 mg sodium

¼ cup drained sun-dried tomatoes packed in oil
6 cups mixed fresh salad greens, roughly torn
½ cup currants
¼ cup coarsely chopped toasted hazelnuts
¼ cup crumbled Oregon blue cheese or other blue cheese

DRESSING
¼ cup balsamic vinegar
¼ cup sugar

Green Salad with Fresh Fennel

The dressing for this salad is so outstanding you'll be happy you have extra to use on another salad!

Yield: 6 servings

In a small bowl, prepare the dressing by whisking all ingredients together.

In a large salad bowl, toss all ingredients with ½ cup of the freshly made dressing. Serve immediately.

Nutrition Facts Per Serving: 227 calories, 18 g total fat (3 g saturated), 8 mg cholesterol, 15 g carbohydrate, 5 g protein, 336 mg sodium

6 cups mixed fresh salad greens, roughly torn
1 bulb fresh fennel, white part only, thinly sliced
¼ cup chopped fresh parsley
½ cup chopped toasted walnuts
½ cup crumbled feta cheese

ORANGE DRESSING
¼ cup olive oil
1 cup freshly squeezed orange juice
⅓ cup freshly squeezed lemon juice
3 cloves garlic, minced
2 teaspoons Dijon mustard
2 teaspoons sugar
3 tablespoons water
1 teaspoon ground cinnamon
¾ teaspoon ground cumin
½ teaspoon salt
½ teaspoon pepper

SPINACH SALAD WITH RASPBERRY-POPPY SEED DRESSING

10 ounces fresh spinach
1 can (11 ounces) mandarin orange
    sections, drained
½ small red onion, thinly sliced
2 tablespoons roasted sunflower
    seeds

RASPBERRY-POPPY SEED
DRESSING
¾ cup sugar
1 teaspoon dry mustard
⅓ cup raspberry vinegar
1 tablespoon finely chopped onion
1 cup vegetable oil
1½ teaspoons poppy seeds

A beautiful, elegant introduction to an evening repast.

Yield: 8 servings

In a food processor, prepare the dressing by combining the first 4 ingredients (sugar through onion) and processing 15 seconds. With motor running, slowly add oil in a steady stream through the feed tube. Add the poppy seeds and pulse once.

Tear spinach into bite-sized pieces. Place in a large serving bowl with remaining ingredients. Toss gently.

To serve, add ¾ cup dressing to the salad; gently toss again to mix.

NOTE
To make raspberry vinegar, see "Medley of Flavored Vinegars" on page 138 in the Gifts section.

Nutrition Facts Per Serving: 358 calories, 29 g total fat (3 g saturated), 0 mg cholesterol, 26 g carbohydrate, 2 g protein, 35 mg sodium

WARM SPINACH SALAD WITH GINGERED SEAFOOD

1 pound fresh scallops, or 1 pound
    fresh shrimp, or 1½ pounds
    fresh mussels
⅓ cup olive oil
2 teaspoons chopped fresh ginger
2 teaspoons minced garlic
1 pound fresh spinach
2 tablespoons freshly squeezed
    lemon juice
Salt and pepper to taste

Sautéed seafood provides a sumptuous surprise to this unique salad.

Yield: 4 servings

Place 4 salad plates in a 200-degree oven to warm.

Prepare seafood (see note).

In a large frying pan, heat olive oil over medium-high heat. Add the seafood, ginger, and garlic. Sauté gently, until scallops or shrimp are cooked, or until mussels are heated through.

Tear spinach into bite-sized pieces. In a large serving bowl, toss spinach with lemon juice; season to taste. Add the seafood with its juices; return mixture to frying pan and toss lightly. Serve immediately on the warmed plates.

NOTE
Scallops need no further preparation; shell and devein shrimp; or scrub mussels, remove beards, steam over boiling water until shells open, and remove meat from shells.

Nutrition Facts Per Serving (using scallops): 287 calories, 19 g total fat (2 g saturated), 37 mg cholesterol, 8 g carbohydrate, 22 g protein, 273 mg sodium

Spinach-Strawberry Salad

A taste of summer sunshine.

Yield: 8 servings

To make dressing, place sugar and lemon juice in a lidded jar and shake until the sugar is dissolved. Add oil; shake well. Refrigerate until needed.

In a small, heavy frying pan, heat the sugar and almonds, stirring constantly until sugar caramelizes. Immediately remove from heat and spread coated nuts on aluminum foil; cool and crumble.

Toss spinach, strawberries, and dressing in a large bowl. Place on plates and sprinkle with sugared almonds.

Nutrition Facts Per Serving: 200 calories, 14 g total fat (1 g saturated), 0 mg cholesterol, 19 g carbohydrate, 3 g protein, 343 mg sodium

10 ounces fresh spinach
1 pound strawberries, hulled and sliced

LEMON DRESSING
¼ cup sugar
Juice of a large lemon (about 3 tablespoons)
6 tablespoons vegetable oil

TOPPING
¼ cup sugar
⅓ cup sliced almonds

Grilled Salmon Louis

The secret of this salad is in the preparation of the romaine.

Yield: 6 servings

Salt and pepper salmon steak. Grill salmon on barbecue until it flakes easily when tested with a fork; cool. Flake the salmon and set aside.

To make the dressing, place olive oil and vinegar in a lidded glass jar. Combine anchovies and garlic to make a paste; add paste to oil and vinegar; shake. Blend in Worcestershire sauce, hot pepper sauce, lemon juice, and water.

Remove and discard the center stem from each lettuce leaf. Tear the remainder of the leaves into bite-sized pieces.

To assemble the salad, place half the Parmesan cheese in a large salad bowl. Layer half the romaine over the cheese. Repeat layers of cheese and lettuce. Add the dressing and croutons. Toss the salad. Add half the salmon and gently toss again. Top salad with remaining salmon.

Nutrition Facts Per Serving: 238 calories, 17 g total fat (3 g saturated), 21 mg cholesterol, 11 g carbohydrate, 12 g protein, 251 mg sodium

6 ounces salmon steak or fillet
Salt and pepper to taste
2 large heads romaine lettuce
½ cup freshly grated Parmesan cheese
Garlic or Caesar croutons

DRESSING
⅓ cup light olive oil
3 tablespoons red wine-garlic vinegar
1 rounded teaspoon well-mashed anchovies (do not substitute anchovy paste)
6 cloves garlic, minced
1 teaspoon Worcestershire sauce
⅛ teaspoon hot pepper sauce
Juice from ½ lemon
2 tablespoons water

8 medium potatoes
⅓ cup chopped onions
½ cup chopped celery
1½ tablespoons fresh basil, chopped
2 teaspoons dill weed
Salt and pepper to taste
4 tablespoons vinegar
½ cup nonfat mayonnaise
Paprika

Portland Potato Salad

This potato salad without eggs tastes even better when you realize how good it is for you.

Yield: 8 servings

In a large saucepan, cook unpeeled potatoes in boiling water until tender. Drain and cool the potatoes slightly; peel and cube.

Combine onions, celery, fresh basil, dill weed, and salt and pepper. In a large salad bowl, layer ¼ of the potatoes; sprinkle with ¼ of the onion-herb mixture and 1 tablespoon vinegar. Repeat layers 3 times. Refrigerate 2 to 3 hours.

Toss with mayonnaise and garnish with a dash of paprika.

Nutrition Facts Per Serving: 118 calories, 1 g total fat (0 g saturated), 0 mg cholesterol, 25 g carbohydrate, 3 g protein, 179 mg sodium

1 pound fresh sugar-snap peas
2 tablespoons vegetable oil
2 teaspoons sesame oil
1 tablespoon hot chili-garlic sauce
1 tablespoon rice vinegar

Sugar-Snap Pea Salad with Hot Chili-Garlic Sauce

A crisp and colorful salad that goes together in a snap!

Yield: 6 servings

Remove the stem end from each sugar-snap pea. Place the peas in a large collander and pour about 2 quarts of boiling water over them, just barely blanching the peas.

Plunge the peas in cold water to set the color and stop the cooking; drain and chill.

To assemble the salad, toss the peas with the oils; then add the hot chili-garlic sauce and vinegar. Toss again to thoroughly coat the peas with the dressing and serve.

If assembling ahead of time, chill the salad up to 2 hours but don't add the vinegar until the last minute. If the salad is allowed to stand, the acid in the vinegar will alter the beautiful color of the peas.

NOTE
Hot chili-garlic sauce is a commercially prepared condiment which is available in the specialty food section of many supermarkets.

Nutrition Facts Per Serving: 91 calories, 6 g total fat (0.8 g saturated), 0 mg cholesterol, 7 g carbohydrate, 2 g protein, 118 mg sodium

Tortellini Garden Salad

Especially good with fresh produce from your own—or your neighbor's— garden!

Yield: 6 servings

Cook tortellini as package directs; drain.

Meanwhile, combine all dressing ingredients in a small bowl.

In a large bowl, combine tortellini with zucchini, tomato, olives, Parmesan cheese, artichoke hearts, and basil.

Add dressing to salad and toss; season to taste. Refrigerate until ready to serve.

NOTE
Adding shrimp to this salad makes a hearty meal.

Nutrition Facts Per Serving: 357 calories, 23 g total fat (5 g saturated), 29 mg cholesterol, 29 g carbohydrate, 9 g protein, 952 mg sodium

8 ounces cheese-filled tortellini
1 zucchini, sliced
1 tomato, diced
½ cup Kalamata or ripe olives, sliced
¼ cup grated Parmesan cheese
1 jar (6 ounces) marinated artichoke hearts, drained and quartered
1 tablespoon chopped fresh basil or 1 teaspoon dried
Salt and pepper to taste

DRESSING
5 tablespoons olive oil
2 tablespoons balsamic vinegar
1 small clove garlic, minced

Ginger-Pasta Salad

Garden-fresh, tasty, and colorful; garnish with nasturtiums for a special occasion. Leftover salad would be wonderful but don't count on it.

Yield: 10 servings

Combine all dressing ingredients in a blender. Process until smooth.

Break angel hair pasta into shorter lengths and cook according to package directions; drain and rinse in cold water. In a large bowl, toss pasta with half of the dressing.

Blanch pea pods in boiling water for 30 seconds; drain and rinse in cold water. Cut pea pods into bite-sized pieces.

Combine pasta and remaining ingredients, except peanuts. Chill until serving time.

To serve, gently toss salad with remaining dressing and peanuts.

VARIATION
Use other shapes of pasta such as rotini or spaghetti.

Nutrition Facts Per Serving: 371 calories, 15 g total fat (2 g saturated), 0 mg cholesterol, 49 g carbohydrate, 14 g protein, 488 mg sodium

12 ounces angel hair pasta
2 cups snow-pea pods, trimmed
2 carrots, thinly sliced
1 red pepper, diced
1 green pepper, diced
1 cup broccoli florets
1 cup cauliflower florets
6 green onions, thinly sliced
1 cup dry-roasted peanuts

DRESSING
½ cup rice vinegar
¼ cup low-sodium soy sauce
¼ cup low-fat peanut butter
2 teaspoons sesame oil
2 tablespoons olive oil
1 tablespoon sugar
1 teaspoon dry mustard
1 teaspoon grated ginger root
1 teaspoon minced garlic
2 tablespoons sesame seeds, toasted

Couscous-Chicken Salad

1 cup orange juice
¾ cup golden raisins
1⅓ cups water
2 teaspoons olive oil
1 package (5.7 ounces) couscous-
    curry mix
1 cup cooked chicken, cut into bite-
    sized pieces
¾ cup frozen petite peas
¾ cup coarsely chopped green
    pepper
¾ cup coarsely chopped celery
3 tablespoons pine nuts
¼ teaspoon salt
⅛ teaspoon pepper
3 tablespoons cider vinegar

Bright and cheery in taste and looks. Best if made at least 8 hours before serving.

Yield: 8 servings

Warm orange juice in microwave for 1½ minutes on full power. Soak raisins in orange juice for 30 minutes or until plump.

In a medium saucepan, combine water, olive oil, and contents of seasoning packet from couscous mix. Bring to a boil; cover and simmer 2 minutes. Stir in couscous; cover and remove from heat. Let stand 5 minutes.

Combine all remaining ingredients, except vinegar, with couscous; sprinkle with vinegar. Stir in raisins and half the orange juice; add enough of the remaining orange juice to moisten salad. Chill until ready to serve.

NOTE

To prepare couscous mix in a microwave, combine water, olive oil, and contents of seasoning packet in a round 2-quart casserole. Cover and microwave on full power for 5 to 6 minutes or until boiling. Stir in couscous, cover, and let stand 5 minutes.

Nutrition Facts Per Serving: 198 calories, 4 g total fat (0.7 g saturated), 15 mg cholesterol, 33 g carbohydrate, 10 g protein, 274 mg sodium

Mandarin Chicken Salad

3 boneless, skinless chicken breast
    halves, cut into 1-inch pieces
1 small red onion, thinly sliced
½ red pepper, thinly sliced
½ green pepper, thinly sliced
1 cup fresh pea pods
1 can (8 ounces) sliced water
    chestnuts, drained
½ cup sliced fresh mushrooms
6 cups mixed salad greens
1 can (11 ounces) mandarin orange
    sections, drained
¼ cup toasted cashew nuts

FRESH GINGER DRESSING
½ cup soy sauce
⅓ cup water
¼ cup honey
1 teaspoon cornstarch
2 cloves garlic, minced
1½ teaspoons grated fresh ginger

Tart and tasty, this versatile chicken salad is destined to become a favorite.

Yield: 6 servings

In a small saucepan, combine all dressing ingredients; mix well. Cook over medium heat for 5 minutes, stirring occasionally. Set aside.

In a large frying pan or wok, sauté chicken in ¼ cup of the dressing until chicken is thoroughly cooked.

Stir in onion, red and green pepper, pea pods, water chestnuts, and mushrooms. Stir-fry about 2 minutes over medium heat, tossing to coat all ingredients.

On a large platter, arrange mixed greens. Top with stir-fry mixture, orange sections, and cashews. Drizzle remaining warm dressing over salad. Serve immediately.

Nutrition Facts Per Serving: 250 calories, 4 g total fat (1 g saturated), 48 mg cholesterol, 31 g carbohydrate, 24 g protein, 1,229 mg sodium

Thai Chicken-Fettucine Salad

Perfect summer fare—casual, but distinctive.

Yield: 4 servings

Cook fettucine as package directs; drain.

Meanwhile, prepare Thai Dressing. Combine all dressing ingredients in a small pan and warm over low heat, stirring until well blended; reserve ¼ cup. Toss fettucine with remainder of the dressing.

In medium frying pan, sauté the chicken in oil about 5 minutes until thoroughly cooked. Add reserved ¼ cup dressing to chicken and mix well.

Toss chicken and fettucine together. Sprinkle with cilantro, peanut halves, and red pepper strips.

Cool in the refrigerator; remove ½ hour before serving to enhance flavors.

Nutrition Facts Per Serving: 577 calories, 28 g total fat (5 g saturated), 50 mg cholesterol, 52 g carbohydrate, 32 g protein, 347 mg sodium

6 ounces dry fettucine
2 tablespoons vegetable oil
3 boneless, skinless chicken breast halves, cut into 1-inch pieces
¼ cup chopped fresh cilantro leaves
¼ cup peanut halves
¼ cup thinly sliced red pepper

THAI DRESSING
1 cup picante salsa
¼ cup chunky peanut butter
2 tablespoons honey
1 teaspoon soy sauce
2 tablespoons orange juice
½ teaspoon ground ginger

Chutney-Chicken Salad

Lime in the dressing adds a unique twist.

Yield: 8 servings

Toss the chicken, pineapple, and green onions together.

Combine dressing ingredients and blend with chicken mixture.

Spoon the salad into lettuce cups and sprinkle with toasted almonds.

Nutrition Facts Per Serving: 221 calories, 6 g total fat (0.8 g saturated), 55 mg cholesterol, 18 g carbohydrate, 24 g protein, 621 mg sodium

4 cups diced, cooked, skinless chicken breast
½ cup fresh pineapple, cut into bite-sized pieces
½ cup thinly sliced green onions
Fresh lettuce cups
½ cup slivered almonds, toasted

CHUTNEY DRESSING
1 cup nonfat mayonnaise
½ cup mango chutney, chopped
¼ cup freshly squeezed lime juice
2 teaspoons freshly grated lime peel
1 teaspoon curry powder
½ teaspoon salt

Oregon is for seafood and fish connoisseurs. The ocean offers salmon, snapper, halibut, ling cod, and shellfish, while rivers and lakes yield six kinds of trout, four kinds of salmon, bass, catfish, and bluegill.

4 cups torn lettuce
1 pound cooked salad shrimp
8 pitted black olives
2 tomatoes, cut into wedges
2 large eggs, hard-cooked, peeled,
    and sliced

EGG DRESSING

1 cup nonfat mayonnaise
1 clove garlic, minced
1 tablespoon chopped fresh parsley
1 tablespoon capers
1 teaspoon freshly squeezed lemon
    juice
2 large eggs, hard-cooked, peeled,
    and chopped
1 teaspoon chopped fresh chives
1 teaspoon chopped fresh dill weed

1 head iceberg lettuce, shredded
    (5–6 cups)
1 can (8 ounces) sliced water
    chestnuts, drained
1 bunch green onions, sliced
¼ pound bean sprouts
2 stalks celery, sliced on the
    diagonal
1 pound cooked salad shrimp
½ pound fresh snow-pea pods,
    blanched
12 cherry tomatoes, halved
1 cup toasted cashews, optional

DRESSING

1 cup low-fat mayonnaise
1 cup low-fat sour cream
2 tablespoons sugar
2 teaspoons curry powder
1 teaspoon ginger
2–3 tablespoons low-fat milk

SHRIMP SALAD PLATE

Sensational salad for seafood lovers.

Yield: 8 servings

To prepare the dressing, mix all its ingredients and chill 2 hours before serving.

Divide the lettuce among 8 salad plates.

Distribute shrimp evenly over the lettuce. Top each salad with 2 tablespoons of the Egg Dressing.

Garnish with olives, tomato wedges, and sliced egg.

VARIATION
Substitute 1 pound crab for shrimp.

Nutrition Facts Per Serving: 137 calories, 4 g total fat (1 g saturated), 217 mg cholesterol, 9 g carbohydrate, 16 g protein, 592 mg sodium

PACIFIC RIM LAYERED SHRIMP SALAD

Use a glass serving bowl so the layers of this beautiful salad can be seen and appreciated.

Yield: 12 servings

In a 4-quart glass salad bowl, spread lettuce evenly. Top with layers of water chestnuts, green onions, bean sprouts, celery, shrimp, and pea pods.

In a small bowl, stir together all dressing ingredients. Spread dressing evenly over pea pods; refrigerate for 12 to 24 hours.

To serve, add layer of halved cherry tomatoes and sprinkle with cashews, if desired. Salad may be tossed before serving or left in layers.

NOTE
Two packages (6 ounces each) frozen snow-pea pods (blanched) may be used in place of fresh pea pods.

Nutrition Facts Per Serving: 268 calories, 14 g total fat (3 g saturated), 75 mg cholesterol, 25 g carbohydrate, 14 g protein, 338 mg sodium

BREADS
AND BRUNCH

BLUEBERRY STREUSEL TEACAKE

1½ cups all-purpose flour
½ cup sugar
1 tablespoon baking powder
¼ teaspoon salt
¼ teaspoon ground cinnamon
⅛ teaspoon ground cloves
½ teaspoon grated lemon peel
⅓ cup cold butter
1 large egg
½ cup milk
½ teaspoon lemon extract
1 teaspoon vanilla extract
1 cup fresh blueberries
Whipped cream, optional

PECAN STREUSEL
½ cup finely chopped pecans
½ cup firmly packed brown sugar
2 tablespoons flour
2 teaspoons ground cinnamon
½ teaspoon grated lemon peel
2 tablespoons butter, melted

Fresh blueberries and pecan streusel dress up this simple butter cake. Fresh wild huckleberries found in the Oregon Cascade mountains could also be used.

Yield: 10 servings

Preheat oven to 350 degrees. Grease and flour a 9-inch round pan with a removable bottom or a springform pan.

In a large bowl, combine flour, sugar, baking powder, spices, and lemon peel. With a pastry blender or 2 knives, cut the butter into the dry ingredients until the mixture resembles coarse crumbs.

In a medium bowl, beat together egg, milk, and flavorings. Blend with flour mixture just until combined. Fold in berries.

Prepare Pecan Streusel by combining all its ingredients with a pastry blender or 2 knives. Press half the streusel into an even layer in the prepared pan. Spread half of the batter over the streusel in the pan. Repeat layers.

Bake at 350 degrees for 45 to 60 minutes, or until cake tester comes out clean. Let cake rest in the pan for 20 minutes, then remove rim and complete cooling.

Serve with whipped cream, if desired.

Nutrition Facts Per Serving (without whipped cream): 375 calories, 13 g total fat (6 g saturated), 45 mg cholesterol, 59 g carbohydrate, 6 g protein, 266 mg sodium

CRANBERRY-DATE BREAD

4½ cups all-purpose flour
2 cups sugar
½ teaspoon salt
2 teaspoons baking powder
2 teaspoons baking soda
2 cups dates, diced
1 pound cranberries, fresh or frozen
1 cup chopped nuts
Grated peel of 4 oranges
4 large eggs, beaten
2 cups buttermilk
1½ cups vegetable oil

SYRUP
½ cup sugar
⅓ cup orange juice

An attractive bread that freezes well. Wonderful for holiday gifts.

Yield: 3 loaves (24 servings)

Preheat oven to 350 degrees. Grease and flour three 9x5-inch loaf pans (or 1 bundt pan and 1 loaf pan).

Sift together the flour, sugar, salt, baking powder, and baking soda.

Add fruits, nuts, and orange peel; toss to coat.

Stir in eggs, buttermilk, and oil with a spoon; do not use an electric mixer.

Spoon the batter into prepared pans. Bake at 350 degrees for 60 minutes, or until the bread is light brown and springs back when lightly touched.

Let bread cool in pans for 10 minutes.

Meanwhile, in a small saucepan, combine syrup ingredients. Bring to a boil to dissolve the sugar.

Turn bread out of the pans and pour an equal amount of syrup over the top of each cooled loaf. Let the bread cool completely before slicing.

Nutrition Facts Per Serving: 404 calories, 18 g total fat (2 g saturated), 36 mg cholesterol, 58 g carbohydrate, 6 g protein, 214 mg sodium

EMON-LIME BREAD

A delightful bread, bright with citrus flavors and the crunch of nuts.

Yield: 1 loaf (14 servings)

Preheat oven to 350 degrees. Grease an 8x4-inch loaf pan.

In a large bowl, cream sugar and butter until fluffy. Add the eggs, mixing well.

Combine flour, baking powder, and salt. Add dry ingredients alternately with milk to the creamed mixture, blending well after each addition. Stir in nuts and grated citrus peels.

Pour batter into prepared loaf pan and bake at 350 degrees for 60 minutes or until done. Remove bread from oven and let it cool in the pan for 10 minutes.

Meanwhile, in a small saucepan, make syrup by combining the lemon and lime juices with sugar. Heat until sugar is dissolved.

While bread is still in the pan, poke holes in the top with a skewer or toothpick. Spoon the syrup over the loaf; leave bread in the pan for 30 minutes before removing it.

Nutrition Facts Per Serving: 231 calories, 11 g total fat (5 g saturated), 49 mg cholesterol, 30 g carbohydrate, 4 g protein, 182 mg sodium

1 cup sugar
½ cup butter
2 large eggs
1¼ cups all-purpose flour
1 teaspoon baking powder
½ teaspoon salt
½ cup milk
¾ cup walnuts, chopped
Grated peel of one lemon
Grated peel of one lime

SYRUP
2 tablespoons freshly squeezed
    lemon juice
2 tablespoons freshly squeezed lime
    juice
5 tablespoons sugar

TRAWBERRY BREAD

This tea bread fills the house with the sweet fragrance of warm strawberries.

Yield: 1 loaf (12 servings)

Preheat oven to 350 degrees. Grease an 8x4-inch loaf pan. Line it with waxed paper and grease the paper.

In a large bowl, cream together butter, sugar, and almond extract. Beat in egg yolks.

Mix in flour, baking powder, and baking soda. Stir in chopped strawberries.

In a separate clean bowl, beat egg whites until stiff; fold into batter. Spoon batter into prepared pan.

Bake at 350 degrees for 50 to 60 minutes, or until cake tester inserted in center comes out clean.

Cool bread on wire rack 15 minutes before removing from pan. Cool completely before slicing.

NOTE
If substituting sweetened, frozen strawberries, thaw completely and drain; reduce sugar to ¾ cup. Bread is prettier using fresh berries.

Nutrition Facts Per Serving: 224 calories, 9 g total fat (5 g saturated), 56 mg cholesterol, 34 g carbohydrate, 3 g protein, 223 mg sodium

½ cup butter
1 cup sugar
½ teaspoon almond extract
2 large eggs, separated
2 cups all-purpose flour
1 teaspoon baking powder
1 teaspoon baking soda
1 cup chopped fresh strawberries

Cranberry Keeping-Cake

The flavor of this delicious holiday cake improves when it is "kept" in a cool, dry place.

Yield: 2 loaves (20 servings)

2½ cups cranberries, divided (if using frozen, do not thaw)
⅔ cup sugar
½ teaspoon grated orange peel
½ cup butter
2¼ cups all-purpose flour, sifted
2 cups firmly packed brown sugar
2 teaspoons ground cinnamon
½ teaspoon ground nutmeg
½ teaspoon ground allspice
¼ teaspoon ground cloves
1 teaspoon salt
2 large eggs
¾ cup sour cream
2 teaspoons baking soda, dissolved in 2 teaspoons water
1 cup coarsely chopped walnuts

Preheat oven to 350 degrees. Grease and flour two 8x4-inch loaf pans.

In a 1-quart saucepan, combine 1¼ cups cranberries, sugar, and orange peel; bring to a boil. Cook, stirring constantly, until berries pop and mixture thickens, about 5 minutes. Remove from heat.

Chop the remaining cranberries coarsely and add to the cranberry mixture. Cool.

Melt the butter over very low heat until creamy, not liquid. Cool.

In a large bowl, sift together the flour, brown sugar, cinnamon, nutmeg, allspice, cloves, and salt.

In another bowl, beat eggs well. Beat in the sour cream, then the dissolved baking soda. Stir egg mixture into sifted dry ingredients just until mixed. Beat in the melted butter, then the cranberry mixture and walnuts.

Pour batter into prepared loaf pans and bake at 350 degrees for 1 hour, or until a cake tester inserted in the center comes out clean.

Cool cakes in pans on a wire rack for 15 minutes; remove cakes from pans and cool completely on wire rack.

Wrap cakes in aluminum foil and allow them to age at least 1 week before serving.

NOTE
The cakes will keep for 3 months in a cool, dry place or the refrigerator. Freeze for longer storage, up to a year; thaw a frozen cake in its wrapper to prevent sogginess.

Nutrition Facts Per Serving: 271 calories, 11 g total fat (4 g saturated), 37 mg cholesterol, 42 g carbohydrate, 4 g protein, 299 mg sodium

Currant-Orange Scones

A light version of scones, with lots of tangy flavor.

Yield: 15 scones

2 cups all-purpose flour
1 tablespoon baking powder
2 tablespoons sugar
½ teaspoon salt
¾ cup currants
3 large egg whites
⅓ cup nonfat yogurt
¼ cup frozen orange juice concentrate, defrosted

Preheat oven to 350 degrees. Lightly grease a baking sheet.

In a medium bowl, combine the flour, baking powder, sugar, and salt. Add currants; stir to mix.

In a separate smaller bowl, beat egg whites with a whisk; add the yogurt and beat again to a frothy mixture. Add the orange juice concentrate and beat again.

Gently fold the liquid mixture into the flour mixture. Drop by tablespoonfuls onto the baking sheet. Bake at 350 degrees for 18 minutes.

Nutrition Facts Per Scone: 102 calories, 0.2 g total fat (0 g saturated), 0 mg cholesterol, 22 g carbohydrate, 3 g protein, 160 mg sodium

Simple Drop Scones

Perfect for coffee, a morning meeting, or an afternoon tea.

Yield: 12 scones

2 cups all-purpose flour
1 tablespoon baking powder
¼ cup sugar
¼ teaspoon salt
½ cup cold butter
2 large eggs, well beaten
½ cup whipping cream
⅓ cup raisins or currants

Preheat oven to 400 degrees. Grease a baking sheet.

In a medium bowl, mix the dry ingredients together. Cut in butter until the mixture resembles coarse crumbs.

In separate bowl, beat eggs and cream together. Pour egg mixture into the flour mixture and stir just until moistened. Gently stir in raisins or currants.

Drop the batter onto prepared baking sheet using a large spoon or a medium ice-cream scoop.

Bake at 400 degrees for 18 to 20 minutes, or until tops are golden brown.

Nutrition Facts Per Scone: 218 calories, 12 g total fat (7 g saturated), 69 mg cholesterol, 24 g carbohydrate, 4 g protein, 227 mg sodium

Maple-Walnut Muffins

Moist and delicious! These will disappear quickly.

Yield: 12 muffins

1½ cups whole wheat flour
½ cup all-purpose flour
3½ teaspoons baking powder
1 teaspoon ground cinnamon
½ teaspoon ground nutmeg
¾ teaspoon salt
1 large egg
1¼ cups milk
⅔ cup maple syrup
3 tablespoons applesauce
1 cup finely chopped walnuts

Preheat oven to 400 degrees. Grease 12 muffin cups.

In a large bowl, mix the flours, baking powder, and spices.

In a medium bowl, whisk egg until frothy. Blend in milk, syrup, and applesauce.

Make a well in the center of dry ingredients. Pour the liquid mixture into the well and blend the batter just until moistened. Gently blend in nuts.

Divide the batter among the prepared muffin cups.

Bake at 400 degrees for 20 minutes.

Nutrition Facts Per Muffin: 205 calories, 8 g total fat (1 g saturated), 21 mg cholesterol, 30 g carbohydrate, 6 g protein, 260 mg sodium

Cougar Claws

1 cup butter
¼ cup warm water (110–115 degrees)
1 package active dry yeast
¼ cup sugar
3 large egg yolks
½ teaspoon salt
1 can (5.5 ounces) evaporated milk
3¼ cups all-purpose flour
1 large egg white
1 cup sliced almonds

ALMOND FILLING
½ cup butter, softened
1¼ cups powdered sugar
8 ounces almond paste
2 large egg whites
⅔ cup all-purpose flour

The rich yeast dough and almond filling are made at least the day before the cougar claws are assembled and baked. Very handy for a holiday breakfast!

Yield: 21 rolls

Melt the butter; set aside to cool to lukewarm.

In a large mixing bowl, dissolve yeast and sugar in warm water. Add the 3 egg yolks, salt, evaporated milk, and melted butter. Add flour and stir to mix well.

Place the dough in a 1-gallon plastic zipper bag; close the bag and refrigerate 24 hours (or up to 3 days) before continuing.

Meanwhile, prepare the filling: In a food processor or mixer, blend softened butter and powdered sugar. Add the almond paste and mix well. Blend in the 2 egg whites, then the flour. Place in a bowl, cover, and refrigerate until needed.

To finish the cougar claws, preheat oven to 350 degrees. Lightly grease 2 baking sheets. Remove the dough from the refrigerator; let rest a few minutes.

On a lightly floured board, roll out dough to a 12x30-inch rectangle. Cut dough lengthwise into 3 equal strips.

Divide the filling into 3 balls; roll into ropes 30 inches long. Place 1 rope in the center of each strip of dough. Fold the sides of the dough strips over the filling ropes, pinching to seal. Cut each filled strip into 7 pieces.

Along 1 long (folded) side of each piece, make cuts every ¾ inch, halfway through the width of the piece. Fan each piece into a curve so the "claws" open. Place on prepared baking sheets.

In a small bowl, beat 1 egg white until foamy and brush a little on top of each roll; sprinkle with sliced almonds.

Bake at 350 degrees for 12 to 15 minutes or until golden brown.

Nutrition Facts Per Roll: 686 calories, 42 g total fat (11 g saturated), 68 mg cholesterol, 67 g carbohydrate, 16 g protein, 215 mg sodium

The central Oregon coast is one of the finest agate-hunting areas in the world. Winter storms uncover great beds of gravel and allow the Pacific Ocean to carry a dazzling variety of agates to shore.

REFRIGERATOR BRAN ROLLS

These wholesome yeast rolls can be mixed the evening before baking.

Yield: 48 rolls

Place shortening, sugar, bran cereal, and salt in large bowl. Add boiling water and stir until the shortening is melted; let cool to lukewarm.

Meanwhile, soften yeast in warm water.

Add beaten eggs and the softened yeast to the cereal mixture.

Stir in half of the flour, mixing well. Stir in the remaining flour. Dough can be refrigerated at this point for up to 24 hours.

Grease 2 baking sheets. Remove the dough from refrigerator and let rise until double in bulk.

Punch down dough and form into 48 balls. Place the balls on prepared baking sheets, leaving room between each ball to allow for rising. Let rise until double.

Preheat oven to 400 degrees. Bake for 15 to 20 minutes or until nicely browned.

Nutrition Facts Per Roll: 120 calories, 5 g total fat (1 g saturated), 9 mg cholesterol, 17 g carbohydrate, 2 g protein, 90 mg sodium

1 cup vegetable shortening
¾ cup sugar
1 cup bran cereal buds
1½ teaspoons salt
1 cup boiling water
1 cup warm water (110–115 degrees)
2 tablespoons active dry yeast
2 large eggs, well beaten
6½ cups all-purpose flour

FEATHER BEDS

As light as their name! Serve plain as dinner rolls or as cinnamon rolls for breakfast.

Yield: 16 rolls

In a large bowl, dissolve yeast in warm milk. Add shortening, egg, salt, and sugar. Mix to melt shortening and combine ingredients. Stir in flour; let rise 1 hour.

Grease a baking sheet.

Roll out the dough on a lightly floured board to ½-inch thickness. Brush with melted butter and cut into 16 squares. Place on the prepared baking sheet; let rise until double in bulk.

Bake at 425 degrees in a preheated oven for 20 minutes or until lightly browned.

CINNAMON ROLL VARIATION

After the first rising, roll out the dough into a rectangle. Combine filling ingredients and spread on the dough. Roll up jellyroll fashion, slice into rolls, and place on greased baking sheet; let rise until double.

Bake at 425 degrees for 20 minutes or until lightly browned.

Nutrition Facts Per Plain Roll: 260 calories, 13 g total fat (6 g saturated), 37 mg cholesterol, 33 g carbohydrate, 4 g protein, 161 mg sodium

1 cup warm milk (110–115 degrees)
1 tablespoon active dry yeast
3 tablespoons vegetable shortening
1 large egg, beaten
½ teaspoon salt
1½ tablespoons sugar
3 cups all-purpose flour
⅓ cup melted butter for shaping

CINNAMON FILLING
⅓ cup melted butter
¾ cup firmly packed brown sugar
1 tablespoon ground cinnamon
⅓ cup raisins
⅓ cup chopped walnuts

½ cup warm water (110–115
   degrees)
1½ teaspoons active dry yeast
2 tablespoons sugar
1 cup buttermilk
⅓ cup vegetable oil
2 teaspoons baking powder
1 teaspoon salt
Pinch of baking soda
3 cups all-purpose flour

 Sourdough Biscuits

Sourdough batter can be stored in the refrigerator for up to two weeks. Bake biscuits just before serving.

Yield: 18 biscuits

In a large bowl, dissolve yeast in warm water. Add the sugar; let it sit for a few minutes until mixture foams. Using a spoon, stir in remaining ingredients; mix well. Cover and refrigerate for up to 2 weeks.

Preheat oven to 400 degrees. Grease a baking sheet.

Measure out the desired amount of dough (1 cup for 6 biscuits). Place the dough on a lightly floured board. Knead 5 to 6 times. Roll out to 1-inch thickness. Cut out biscuits and place them on greased baking sheet.

Bake at 400 degrees for 15 minutes.

Nutrition Facts Per Biscuit: 124 calories, 4 g total fat (0.6 g saturated), 0 mg cholesterol, 18 g carbohydrate, 3 g protein, 174 mg sodium

½ cup unbleached all-purpose flour
½ cup whole wheat flour
1 cup rolled oats
¼ teaspoon salt
1 teaspoon baking soda
1 tablespoon sugar
1 teaspoon ground cinnamon
¼ cup butter
¾ cup raisins
½ cup buttermilk

Cinnamon-Oat Bars

A wholesome, whole-grain snack bread.

Yield: 8 snack bars

Preheat oven to 400 degrees. Grease a baking sheet.

In a large bowl, combine dry ingredients (flour through cinnamon), mixing well.

Cut in butter with pastry blender or 2 knives until mixture resembles coarse crumbs; then mix in raisins. Stir in buttermilk to make a soft dough.

On a floured board, pat down dough to make a rectangle about ½-inch thick. Cut into eighths. Place bars on prepared baking sheet.

Bake at 400 degrees for 15 minutes.

Nutrition Facts Per Bar: 197 calories, 7 g total fat (4 g saturated), 16 mg cholesterol, 31 g carbohydrate, 4 g protein, 301 mg sodium

SUNRISE CRUNCH GRANOLA

A winning combination of grains, nuts, and fruit.

Yield: 40 half-cup servings

Preheat oven to 250 degrees. Lightly spray 2 large rimmed baking sheets with vegetable spray.

In a large bowl, combine the first 8 ingredients (oats through coconut); mix well.

In a medium saucepan, combine sauce ingredients and heat over medium heat until butter melts; stir to blend.

Drizzle sauce over dry ingredients; mix until all are coated with the sauce.

Spread granola in a thin layer on prepared baking sheets. Bake at 250 degrees for 25 minutes; remove from oven and stir to turn granola completely.

Return to oven, rotating pans if using 2 racks. Bake 20 minutes longer.

Turn oven off, leaving oven door closed. Let granola cool several hours or overnight in oven.

Add 1 cup dried fruit to each pan; mix well. Transfer granola to airtight container.

Nutrition Facts Per Serving: 154 calories, 8 g total fat (3 g saturated), 7 mg cholesterol, 19 g carbohydrate, 4 g protein, 30 mg sodium

6 cups rolled oats, rolled wheat flakes, or 7-grain cereal
¼ cup dried milk powder
½ cup raw wheat germ
½ cup raw sesame seeds
½ cup raw chopped almonds
½ cup raw chopped cashews
½ cup raw peanuts
1 cup flaked coconut
2 cups raisins, chopped dates, other dried fruit, or a combination

SAUCE
½ cup butter
⅓ cup honey
1 teaspoon vanilla extract
¼ teaspoon ground cinnamon

FRUITY OATMEAL CASSEROLE

This oatmeal, thick with fruits and nuts and baked in a casserole, is a hearty addition to the brunch table.

Yield: 8 servings

Preheat oven to 350 degrees. Grease a 2-quart casserole.

In a 2-quart saucepan, combine milk, sugar, butter, salt, and cinnamon; bring to a boil. Stir in remaining ingredients, mixing well.

Pour mixture into the prepared casserole. Bake, uncovered, at 350 degrees for 30 minutes. Stir after 15 minutes to distribute the apples.

Provide individual bowls and plenty of garnishes, such as butter, sugars, honey or maple syrup, and milk or cream.

Nutrition Facts Per Serving (without garnish): 300 calories, 13 g total fat (5 g saturated), 24 mg cholesterol, 40 g carbohydrate, 10 g protein, 432 mg sodium

4 cups milk
½ cup firmly packed brown sugar
2 tablespoons butter
½ teaspoon salt
1 tablespoon ground cinnamon
2 cups old-fashioned oats
2 cups chopped, peeled green apples
½ cup currants or golden raisins
½ cup chopped walnuts
½ cup dried cranberries or dried cherries

GARNISH
Butter
Sugars
Honey or maple syrup
Milk or cream

Sherried French Toast

½ cup 2 percent milk
¼ cup medium-dry sherry
¼ cup sugar
Dash of salt
Grated peel of 1 lemon
8 slices (1-inch thick) firm white
    bread or French bread
2 tablespoons butter
3 large eggs, well-beaten

GARNISH
Butter
Powdered sugar
Ground cinnamon
Freshly squeezed lemon juice

Lemon and sherry dress up French toast to make breakfast a special occasion.

Yield: 4 servings

In a 9x13-inch baking dish, combine the milk, sherry, sugar, salt, and lemon peel. Soak the bread slices in the mixture for several minutes; lift and drain.

Heat a griddle to medium heat and melt the butter on it.

Dip both sides of each bread slice in beaten egg and drain; then cook on hot griddle until browned, turning once.

Serve while hot and pass the butter, powdered sugar, cinnamon, and lemon juice.

Nutrition Facts Per Serving (without garnish): 324 calories, 11 g total fat (5 g saturated), 177 mg cholesterol, 41 g carbohydrate, 10 g protein, 426 mg sodium

Oregon Trail Fritters

1 cup unbleached whole wheat flour
1 large egg, beaten
Pinch of salt
1 cup lager (beer)
2 large firm apples, peeled, cored,
    and cut into bite-sized pieces
⅓ cup dried cranberries
⅔ cup golden raisins
3–5 cups oil for frying

TOPPING
½ cup powdered sugar
1 teaspoon ground cinnamon

The bounty of Oregon to nourish the pioneer in you!

Yield: 6 servings

In a large bowl, mix the flour, egg, and salt. Add lager; stir just enough to moisten but do not overbeat. Gently fold in fruit.

Heat the oil in a large frying pan over medium-high heat.

Carefully drop large spoonfuls of batter in the oil, allowing generous space between fritters. Fry until golden brown, turning once. Drain on paper towels. Repeat until all batter is used. If batter thickens, add additional lager.

Combine sugar and cinnamon. Sprinkle over hot fritters and serve.

Nutrition Facts Per Fritter: 250 calories, 5 g total fat (0.8 g saturated), 35 mg cholesterol, 48 g carbohydrate, 5 g protein, 16 mg sodium

Agricultural and range lands cover approximately 46% of Oregon's total area, while forests account for another 46%. Deserts cover about 6%, bodies of water 1%, and urban areas less than 1%.

Coastal Crab Quiche

A crustless quiche that assembles quickly, then aptly serves as entrée or appetizer.

Yield: 6 servings

Preheat oven to 350 degrees. Grease a 9-inch round baking dish.

In a medium frying pan, sauté mushrooms in butter; drain.

In a medium bowl, combine the next seven ingredients (eggs through hot pepper sauce). Stir in the mushrooms and grated cheeses; fold in crab.

Pour into the prepared baking dish. Bake at 350 degrees for 45 minutes. Let stand 5 minutes before serving.

NOTE
For an appetizer, bake in a 9-inch square pan, cool, and cut into 1-inch squares.

Nutrition Facts Per Serving: 419 calories, 28 g total fat (16 g saturated), 239 mg cholesterol, 10 g carbohydrate, 32 g protein, 865 mg sodium

2 tablespoons butter
½ pound mushrooms, sliced
4 large eggs, beaten
1 cup small-curd cottage cheese
1 cup sour cream
¼ cup flour
1 teaspoon onion powder
½ teaspoon salt
4 drops hot pepper sauce
2 cups grated Monterey Jack cheese
½ cup freshly grated Parmesan cheese
½ pound crab meat

Petite Petal Quiches

Wonton skins look like little flowers when pressed into mini-muffin pans. These bite-sized quiches are decked out for brunch or as appetizers.

Yield: 24 mini-quiches

Preheat oven to 350 degrees. Spray mini-muffin tins with vegetable spray.

In a small bowl, beat together eggs and cream; set aside.

Press wonton skins into prepared muffin pans. Fill each with a choice of cheese and fillings. Carefully spoon egg mixture into each cup and top with sliced green onions.

Bake at 350 degrees for 15 minutes or until set. Cool a few minutes before removing from pans.

NOTE
Wonton skins can be found in the produce section of most grocery stores. If round wonton skins are not available, cut square ones with a biscuit cutter.

Nutrition Facts Per Quiche: 66 calories, 3 g total fat (2 g saturated), 26 mg cholesterol, 6 g carbohydrate, 3 g protein, 91 mg sodium

2 large eggs
¾ cup half-and-half cream
1 package round wonton skins
¾ cup assorted grated cheeses
4–6 slices bacon, fried and crumbled, or ¾ cup assorted fillings, such as tiny shrimp, chopped broccoli, or crab
2 green onions, sliced

1 pound fresh asparagus, cut into
    bite-sized pieces
¼ cup chopped onion
½ teaspoon sugar
Pinch of salt
3 tablespoons water
6 large eggs, beaten
½ cup evaporated skim milk
½ teaspoon salt
1 cup cooked salad shrimp, optional
1 cup grated Monterey Jack cheese
½ cup grated Cheddar cheese

ASPARAGUS-CHEESE BAKE

A deliciously elegant vegetarian dish for family or guests.

Yield: 6 servings

Preheat oven to 425 degrees.

Generously coat a nonstick frying pan with vegetable spray. Sauté the asparagus and onion 1 minute.

Add sugar, pinch of salt, and water; simmer until all the water evaporates, then cool.

Coat an 8x8-inch microwave dish with vegetable spray.

In a small bowl, combine eggs, milk, and salt; pour into the prepared dish and microwave on full power until the eggs on the bottom of dish are set.

Arrange asparagus mixture and shrimp, if used, over eggs; bake at 425 degrees for 5 minutes. Cover with grated cheeses and bake 10 minutes longer.

Nutrition Facts Per Serving (with shrimp): 244 calories, 14 g total fat (7 g saturated), 277 mg cholesterol, 7 g carbohydrate, 21 g protein, 486 mg sodium

4 cups cubed, day-old, firm white
    bread
2 cups (8 ounces) shredded
    Cheddar cheese
10 large eggs, lightly beaten
1 quart 1 percent milk
1 teaspoon dry mustard
1 teaspoon salt
Pepper to taste
¼ teaspoon onion powder
½ cup sliced mushrooms
½ cup chopped, peeled, and seeded
    tomato
8 slices cooked bacon, crumbled

TOMATO-MUSHROOM SOUFFLÉ

This dish is prepared in advance—eggs, bacon, and bread all in one dish.

Yield: 10 servings

Generously grease a 9x13-inch baking pan. Arrange bread cubes in prepared pan; sprinkle with cheese.

In a medium bowl, beat together the eggs, milk, and seasonings; pour evenly over the bread cubes. Top with the mushrooms, tomato, and bacon.

Cover with plastic wrap; chill overnight or up to 24 hours.

Preheat oven to 325 degrees. Bake, uncovered, for 1 hour or until set.

VARIATION
Instead of bacon, 6 ounces of sausage, cooked and crumbled, may be used.

Nutrition Facts Per Serving: 424 calories, 18 g total fat (8 g saturated), 245 mg cholesterol, 43 g carbohydrate, 22 g protein, 1,311 mg sodium

Western Baked Eggs

All the goodness of a hearty country breakfast combined in this brunch dish.

Yield: 8 servings

Preheat oven to 350 degrees. Grease a 9x13-inch baking dish.

In a large frying pan, brown potatoes, onions, and parsley in oil over medium heat. Transfer to the prepared baking dish.

In a medium saucepan, melt butter; stir in flour, salt, and pepper. Add milk slowly and cook over low heat, stirring constantly until thickened. Remove from heat; stir in sour cream. Pour sauce over the potatoes, lifting potatoes lightly to permit sauce to mix well.

Bake at 350 degrees for 30 minutes.

Remove from oven. Make 8 indentations in the potatoes using the back of a large spoon. Slip an egg into each indentation and season each with salt and pepper.

Bake 10 to 15 minutes more, or until eggs are set as desired.

Nutrition Facts Per Serving: 307 calories, 22 g total fat (10 g saturated), 247 mg cholesterol, 18 g carbohydrate, 11 g protein, 469 mg sodium

2 tablespoons vegetable oil
4 cups shredded cooked potatoes
½ cup chopped onion
2 tablespoons chopped fresh parsley
¼ cup butter
½ cup all-purpose flour
1 teaspoon salt
¼ teaspoon pepper
1½ cups milk
1 cup sour cream
8 large eggs
Salt and pepper to taste

Herbed Eggs in a Nest

Creamy scrambled eggs in a nest of sausage and potatoes.

Yield: 8 servings

Peel and grate potatoes; plunge them immediately into salted ice water. Pour potatoes into colander to remove water; set aside.

In a large, nonstick frying pan, sauté garlic, onions, and mushrooms in 2 tablespoons oil until softened. Add grated potatoes and brown on one side. Add sausage; turn with large spatula to brown on other side. Repeat, if necessary, until all potatoes are well-browned and crisp. Season with lemon pepper, parsley, chives, and ½ teaspoon salt. Turn out onto platter and place in warm oven while eggs are prepared.

Wipe frying pan clean and add 1 tablespoon oil. Scramble eggs over low heat; add cubes of cream cheese, stirring slightly to mix. Remove from heat and season with salt and pepper to taste. Turn out onto potatoes and garnish with tomato and chopped cilantro or parsley; serve with salsa if desired.

Nutrition Facts Per Serving: 217 calories, 15 g total fat (4 g saturated), 120 mg cholesterol, 14 g carbohydrate, 8 g protein, 391 mg sodium

4 large potatoes
3 tablespoons vegetable oil, divided
1 clove garlic, minced
1 onion, thinly sliced
1 cup sliced mushrooms
4 ounces lean turkey kielbasa
    sausage, peeled and chopped
¼ teaspoon lemon pepper
1 tablespoon chopped fresh parsley
½ tablespoon minced chives
½ teaspoon salt
4 large eggs, lightly beaten
¼ cup low-fat cream cheese, cubed
Salt and pepper to taste
1 large tomato, peeled and chopped
⅓ cup chopped fresh cilantro leaves
    or parsley
Prepared salsa, optional

APPLE-RAISIN COMPOTE

2 tablespoons butter
3 medium cooking apples, peeled and thinly sliced
½ cup raisins
¼ teaspoon ground cinnamon
¼ teaspoon ground nutmeg
2 tablespoons maple syrup

Surprise them at breakfast with a new topping for pancakes, waffles, or French toast.

Yield: 4 servings

In a medium frying pan, sauté apples, raisins, and spices in butter for 10 minutes. Add syrup and cook 5 minutes over medium heat.

Nutrition Facts Per Serving: 192 calories, 6 g total fat (4 g saturated), 15 mg cholesterol, 37 g carbohydrate, 1 g protein, 61 mg sodium

FROZEN FRUIT COMPOTE

3 bananas, peeled and diced
2 cans (10 ounces each) crushed pineapple with juice
3 cups sliced strawberries
12 ounces frozen passion-orange-guava juice concentrate, thawed
32 ounces lemon-lime soda

GARNISH
Strawberries, mint leaves, or fresh flowers

Make extra…even the children will be asking for seconds.

Yield: 8 servings

Thoroughly mix fruit with juice concentrate. Gently stir in soda. Place in a large freezer container that allows room for expansion and cover tightly. Freeze until firm.

Remove from freezer 1½ hours before serving and let stand at room temperature.

Using a metal spoon, crush the fruit mixture and scoop into compote dishes to serve. Garnish with fresh strawberries, mint leaves, or fresh flowers.

Nutrition Facts Per Serving: 226 calories, 0.5 g total fat (0.1 g saturated), 0 mg cholesterol, 58 g carbohydrate, 1 g protein, 14 mg sodium

RUBY COMPOTE

8 ounces whole-berry cranberry sauce
2 tablespoons honey
1 tablespoon freshly squeezed lemon juice
¼ teaspoon ground cinnamon
¼ teaspoon ground ginger
3 fresh pears, peeled, cored, and cut into bite-sized pieces
2 oranges, peeled and cut up
1 cup seedless green grapes, halved
½ cup seedless red grapes, halved

A fruitful combination of color—nice as a winter fruit cup or a meat accompaniment.

Yield: 6 servings

In a medium saucepan, combine the cranberry sauce, honey, lemon juice, and spices. Bring to a boil, then reduce heat to simmer.

Add pears to the sauce and simmer until tender.

Add oranges and grapes and simmer until heated through.

Serve compote warm or chilled.

Nutrition Facts Per Serving: 184 calories, 0.7 g total fat (0 g saturated), 0 mg cholesterol, 50 g carbohydrate, 1 g protein, 15 mg sodium

Entrées

¼ cup butter, melted
1 teaspoon celery salt
1 teaspoon paprika
1 teaspoon salt
½ teaspoon dried oregano
½ teaspoon pepper
¼ teaspoon curry powder
½ cup all-purpose flour
8 boneless, skinless chicken breast
    halves
½ cup sliced almonds
1 cup 1 percent milk
½ cup low-fat sour cream
½ cup dry sherry, optional

Sour Cream-Almond Chicken

Pretty and sophisticated...healthful as well.

Yield: 8 servings

Preheat oven to 350 degrees.

In a medium bowl, blend butter and seasonings. Dredge each piece of chicken in flour, dip in seasoned butter, and place in an ovenproof casserole.

Sprinkle with almonds. Pour milk over the chicken; cover and bake at 350 degrees for 1 hour.

Reduce oven temperature to 300 degrees. Thin the sour cream with some of the pan juices and sherry, if used; pour over chicken. Bake 20 minutes, uncovered.

Nutrition Facts Per Serving: 268 calories, 13 g total fat (5 g saturated), 69 mg cholesterol, 10 g carbohydrate, 24 g protein, 608 mg sodium

12 boneless, skinless chicken breast
    halves
¼ teaspoon salt
⅛ teaspoon pepper
24 sheets phyllo dough, thawed
1½ cups butter, melted
⅓ cup freshly grated Parmesan
    cheese

LEMON-TARRAGON
SAUCE
1½ cups nonfat mayonnaise
⅓ cup freshly squeezed lemon juice
1 cup chopped green onion
2 cloves garlic, finely minced
2 teaspoons dried tarragon

Chicken Breasts in Phyllo

This delicately seasoned chicken can be baked immediately or frozen for future use.

Yield: 12 servings

In small bowl, combine all Lemon-Tarragon Sauce ingredients. Let stand 10 minutes to allow flavors to develop.

Preheat oven to 375 degrees.

Season chicken lightly with salt and pepper.

Unroll phyllo gently; cover it with waxed paper and a damp towel to prevent drying.

Brush 1 sheet phyllo with melted butter. Place a second sheet on top and brush it with melted butter.

Spread 1½ tablespoons Lemon-Tarragon Sauce on each side of a chicken breast. Place the breast on 1 corner of phyllo sheets; fold 2 sides of phyllo over chicken, roll up to make a packet, using melted butter to seal. Repeat with remaining chicken breasts.

Place sealed packets on ungreased jellyroll pan and brush with remaining butter; sprinkle with grated Parmesan cheese.

Bake at 375 degrees for 35 to 40 minutes or until browned.

NOTE
For future use, wrap the unbaked chicken packets in plastic or foil and freeze. Thaw completely before baking.

Nutrition Facts Per Serving: 388 calories, 20 g total fat (11 g saturated), 94 mg cholesterol, 28 g carbohydrate, 24 g protein, 865 mg sodium

CHICKEN WITH ORANGE SLICES

Citrus slices accentuate the bright flavors in this sauce.

Yield: 4 servings

Preheat oven to 350 degrees.

Salt and pepper the chicken. Dredge in flour

In a large sauté pan over medium heat, lightly brown the chicken breasts in vegetable oil. Remove to a 3-quart casserole.

Drain fat from pan. Add remaining ingredients, except the orange slices, and simmer 2 to 3 minutes. Pour sauce over the chicken.

Cover and bake at 350 degrees for 50 to 60 minutes, or until chicken is tender. Garnish with the orange slices and serve.

Nutrition Facts Per Serving: 302 calories, 15 g total fat (2 g saturated), 51 mg cholesterol, 18 g carbohydrate, 22 g protein, 513 mg sodium

4 boneless, skinless chicken breast halves
Salt and pepper to taste
¼ cup all-purpose flour
¼ cup vegetable oil
1 cup freshly squeezed orange juice
⅓ cup chili sauce
¼ cup chopped green pepper
1 teaspoon prepared mustard
1 teaspoon garlic salt
2 teaspoons soy sauce
1 teaspoon molasses
1 orange, peeled and sliced, for garnish

CURRIED CHICKEN WITH PEARS

A meal in itself, complete with stuffing, fruit, and nuts.

Yield: 6 servings

In a large skillet, brown both sides of chicken breasts in oil over medium heat. Season with the garlic, curry powder, salt, and pepper. Pour in the cider; cover and simmer 10 minutes, basting with the cider once or twice. Remove the cover; stir in seasoning packet from stuffing mix. Add the pears and simmer another 5 minutes to reduce the sauce.

Remove chicken to a warm platter. Stir stuffing mix into the reduced sauce. Add the nuts and mix well. Cover and let stand for 5 minutes. Spoon prepared stuffing mix onto a serving platter and top with the chicken breasts.

VARIATION
Chicken-flavored rice, prepared as package directs, can be substituted for the stuffing in this recipe.

Nutrition Facts Per Serving: 326 calories, 8 g total fat (1 g saturated), 52 mg cholesterol, 39 g carbohydrate, 25 g protein, 903 mg sodium

1 tablespoon olive oil
6 boneless, skinless chicken breast halves
1 clove garlic, minced
1 teaspoon curry powder
¼ teaspoon salt
¼ teaspoon pepper
2 cups apple cider
1 package (6 servings) chicken-flavored stuffing mix
2 firm pears, peeled, cored, and thinly sliced
¼ cup pecan or walnut halves

Apricot-Glazed Chicken

6 boneless, skinless chicken breast
    halves
¾ cup light apricot preserves
½ cup catsup
1 tablespoon minced onion

We won't tell how easy this is to make if you won't.

Yield: 6 servings

Broil or grill chicken until browned.

Preheat oven to 375 degrees.

Place the browned chicken breasts in a baking pan or casserole.

In a small bowl, combine the remaining ingredients; spread mixture over the chicken.

Bake at 375 degrees for 45 minutes or until just cooked through, basting several times with the glaze.

Nutrition Facts Per Serving: 229 calories, 3 g total fat (1 g saturated), 96 mg cholesterol, 15 g carbohydrate, 39 g protein, 350 mg sodium

Chicken and Bok Choy

2 boneless, skinless chicken breast
    halves
2 tablespoons cornstarch, divided
2 tablespoons soy sauce, divided
1 clove garlic, minced
1 pound fresh bok choy cabbage
1 cup water
3 tablespoons vegetable oil, divided
1 inch fresh ginger root, peeled and
    minced
1 medium onion, cut into 1-inch
    chunks
12 cherry tomatoes, halved
½ cup roasted peanuts

Rice is a natural accompaniment for this quick stir-fry dish flavored with ginger and roasted peanuts.

Yield: 4 servings

Cut chicken breasts into thin strips. In a medium bowl, combine 1 tablespoon cornstarch, 1 tablespoon soy sauce, and garlic. Add chicken and marinate until stir-fry stage of preparation.

Slice bok choy crosswise into 1-inch pieces. Separate greens from stalks.

In a small bowl, combine 1 tablespoon soy sauce, 1 tablespoon cornstarch, and water; set aside.

In a wok or large frying pan, heat 2 tablespoons of the oil over high heat. Add chicken and stir-fry 1 minute; remove chicken.

Add remaining 1 tablespoon oil and ginger root to pan; sauté 15 seconds. Add bok choy stalk pieces and onion; sauté 3 minutes, stirring constantly. Add the bok choy greens and stir-fry 1 minute.

Stir in the soy-water mixture, chicken, and tomato halves. Cook until mixture thickens, about 1 minute. Stir in peanuts just to heat through. Serve immediately.

Nutrition Facts Per Serving: 396 calories, 22 g total fat (3 g saturated), 26 mg cholesterol, 36 g carbohydrate, 21 g protein, 570 mg sodium

CHICKEN PACIFICA

An outstanding entrée which demonstrates that "easy" need not be boring.

Yield: 10 servings

In a plastic bag, combine flour, salt, pepper, and thyme.

Rinse chicken, pat dry, and toss in flour mixture until coated.

Heat butter in a large skillet. Brown chicken on all sides.

Add cheese, ham, mushrooms, pineapple, and juice. Reduce heat, cover, and simmer 30 minutes. Uncover; cook another 10 minutes.

If desired, thicken juices with additional flour.

Nutrition Facts Per Serving: 268 calories, 12 g total fat (6 g saturated), 88 mg cholesterol, 10 g carbohydrate, 28 g protein, 903 mg sodium

½ cup all-purpose flour
2 teaspoons salt
½ teaspoon pepper
½ teaspoon thyme
10 boneless, skinless chicken breast halves
¼ cup butter
1 cup grated Cheddar cheese
½ pound cooked lean ham, cubed
¾ cup sliced fresh mushrooms
1 cup drained pineapple chunks
¼ cup pineapple juice

PARMESAN-HERB CHICKEN

This oven-baked chicken with a crunchy crust is a nice change from fried chicken.

Yield: 6 servings

Preheat oven to 300 degrees. Mix bread crumbs, cheese, salt, and parsley.

In a small saucepan, melt butter; add garlic, mustard, and Worcestershire sauce.

Dip chicken in butter mixture, then in seasoned crumbs. Place in a large, shallow baking pan, and drizzle with any remaining butter.

Bake at 300 degrees for 1¼ hours; garnish with chopped parsley.

Nutrition Facts Per Serving: 356 calories, 20 g total fat (11 g saturated), 112 mg cholesterol, 12 g carbohydrate, 31 g protein, 842 mg sodium

¾ cup dry bread crumbs
½ cup grated Parmesan cheese
1 teaspoon salt
⅓ cup chopped fresh parsley
½ cup butter
1 clove garlic, minced
1 teaspoon Dijon mustard
1½ teaspoons Worcestershire sauce
6 boneless, skinless chicken breast halves
Additional chopped parsley, for garnish

Albany, in the mid-Willamette Valley, boasts Oregon's largest variety of architectural styles, with nearly 700 historic churches, homes, and other buildings.

2 tablespoons butter
1 teaspoon lemon juice
4 medium salmon steaks
1 teaspoon dried dill weed

DILL SAUCE
½ cup low-fat mayonnaise
¼ cup low-fat sour cream
1 tablespoon lemon juice
2 teaspoons dried dill weed
½ teaspoon sugar

Salmon Steaks with Dill Sauce

Salmon cooked in a microwave oven is especially tender and perfectly moist. The low-fat sauce ensures a healthful main dish.

Yield: 4 servings

Combine all ingredients for Dill Sauce in a small bowl and mix well. Refrigerate until serving time.

In a small bowl, melt butter in a microwave oven; add lemon juice.

Arrange salmon steaks in a microwave dish. Brush salmon with lemon butter. Cover lightly. Cook at 50 percent power for 5 to 6 minutes. Turn salmon over; brush again with lemon butter. Cover and cook 5 to 6 minutes longer at 50 percent power, or until fish flakes easily. Sprinkle with 1 teaspoon dill weed.

Serve with Dill Sauce.

Nutrition Facts Per Serving: 224 calories, 12 g total fat (5 g saturated), 88 mg cholesterol, 6 g carbohydrate, 24 g protein, 293 mg sodium

½ cup firmly packed brown sugar
1 tablespoon ground allspice
1 tablespoon Dijon mustard
1 tablespoon grated fresh ginger
4 salmon steaks, 1-inch thick
4 lemon slices for garnish

DILLED CUCUMBER
SAUTÉ
1 medium cucumber
1 bunch green onions
2 tablespoons butter
1 tablespoon lemon juice
2 teaspoons dried dill weed
1 tablespoon chopped fresh parsley
Salt and pepper to taste

Ginger Salmon with Dilled Cucumber Sauté

A spectacular way to serve salmon—the seasoned rub really makes it unique.

Yield: 4 servings

In a small bowl, combine brown sugar, allspice, mustard, and ginger. Rub the mixture into both sides of the salmon steaks. Refrigerate at least 1 hour.

Meanwhile, prepare the Dilled Cucumber Sauté. Peel the cucumber and slice lengthwise into quarters; remove the seeds and cut quarters into 1-inch pieces. Slice onions into 1-inch pieces. In a medium saucepan, cook the vegetables with the butter and lemon juice for 10 minutes or until tender yet crisp. Add herbs and season to taste.

Preheat broiler or grill. Cook the salmon steaks about 6 minutes on each side, or until fish flakes easily. Do not overcook.

Garnish each serving with a lemon slice and pass the Dilled Cucumber Sauté.

Nutrition Facts Per Serving: 348 calories, 12 g total fat (5 g saturated), 104 mg cholesterol, 25 g carbohydrate, 36 g protein, 237 mg sodium

FAST FIESTA COD

Serve these spicy fish fillets with the "Savory Black Beans and Rice" on page 102 for a hearty meal.

Yield: 4 servings

Brush fillets with olive oil. Place in microwave dish.

Combine seasonings. Sprinkle each fillet with ½ teaspoon of the spice mixture; cover fish fillets.

Microwave on full power for 2 to 3 minutes, or until fish flakes easily. Remove from microwave and let stand 2 minutes before serving.

Garnish with lime wedges and salsa.

Nutrition Facts Per Serving: 130 calories, 2 g total fat (0.3 g saturated), 61 mg cholesterol, 1 g carbohydrate, 26 g protein, 347 mg sodium

4 cod fillets (about 20 ounces total)
1 teaspoon olive oil
1 teaspoon ground cumin
½ teaspoon chili powder
½ teaspoon garlic powder
⅛ teaspoon cayenne pepper
½ teaspoon salt

GARNISH
Lime wedges
Prepared salsa

RED SNAPPER WITH PARMESAN-CRUMB TOPPING

Any firm fish fillet may be used in this quickly prepared entrée.

Yield: 4 servings

Preheat oven to 350 degrees. Grease a 9x13-inch baking dish or shallow casserole.

In a small frying pan, lightly sauté onion and mushrooms in butter; set aside.

Arrange fish fillets in prepared baking dish; season with salt and paprika.

In a medium bowl, combine sour cream and the mushroom mixture; spread over fish. Sprinkle grated cheese and bread crumbs over the sauce. Bake at 350 degrees for 20 minutes, or until fish flakes easily and crumbs are golden brown. Garnish with chopped parsley and tomato wedges.

Nutrition Facts Per Serving: 229 calories, 11 g total fat (6 g saturated), 72 mg cholesterol, 7 g carbohydrate, 24 g protein, 487 mg sodium

1 tablespoon butter
¼ cup chopped onion
½ cup sliced mushrooms
1 pound fresh red snapper fillets
½ teaspoon salt
½ teaspoon paprika
½ cup sour cream
3 tablespoons freshly grated
    Parmesan cheese
2 tablespoons soft bread crumbs

GARNISH
Chopped fresh parsley
Fresh tomato wedges

MOUNTAIN TROUT WITH SHRIMP STUFFING

½ cup sliced fresh mushrooms
¼ cup diced celery
¼ cup sliced green onions
¼ cup butter, divided
1 cup bread cubes
4 ounces cooked salad shrimp
½ teaspoon salt
½ teaspoon lemon pepper
½ teaspoon dried thyme
¼ cup chicken broth
4 trout (8 ounces each), pan-dressed

If you don't have a fisherman in your family, you can often buy fresh trout at your local seafood market.

Yield: 4 servings

Preheat oven to 350 degrees. Grease a 9x13-inch baking pan.

In a large frying pan, sauté mushrooms, celery, and onions in 2 tablespoons butter for 3 to 4 minutes. Add bread cubes, shrimp, and seasonings; mix well. Stir in chicken broth to bind mixture.

Stuff the cavity of each trout with ¼ of the mixture; place trout in prepared baking pan. Melt remaining 2 tablespoons butter and brush it over the trout.

Bake at 350 degrees for 25 to 30 minutes, or until fish flakes easily. Remove the skin before serving, if desired.

Nutrition Facts Per Serving: 464 calories, 21 g total fat (6 g saturated), 175 mg cholesterol, 12 g carbohydrate, 52 g protein, 653 mg sodium

TANAKU HALIBUT

4 pounds halibut fillets
1½ cups chopped onions
½ teaspoon seafood seasoning
¼ teaspoon curry powder
¼ cup butter
1 cup sliced mushrooms
1 cup grated low-fat Cheddar cheese
1 can (10.7 ounces) cream of
    mushroom soup
1½ cups low-fat sour cream

Enjoy the bounty of the sea accompanied by a unique sauce.

Yield: 12 servings

Preheat oven to 325 degrees.

Cut fish into 1½-inch pieces; place in 9x13-inch baking dish.

Sprinkle onions and seasonings over fish. Dot with butter. Cover with some of the mushrooms, then the grated cheese.

In a medium bowl, combine mushroom soup, the rest of the mushrooms, and the sour cream. Spread over fish.

Bake, uncovered, at 325 degrees for 45 minutes.

Nutrition Facts Per Serving: 254 calories, 9 g total fat (3 g saturated), 63 mg cholesterol, 3 g carbohydrate, 35 g protein, 367 mg sodium

Company's Coming Scampi

Serve this light, quickly sautéed entrée with pasta.

Yield: 6 servings

Shell and devein prawns; leave tails on.

Mash the garlic with the salt to form a paste.

In a large frying pan, heat the butter and oil over medium-high heat. Add the lemon juice, garlic paste, and wine; heat until alcohol cooks off, about 1 minute.

Add the mushrooms and green onion; cook 1 to 2 minutes. Add the prawns; cook on both sides until they are opaque and firm. Do not overcook.

Remove pan from heat and stir in tomato just to heat through. Toss with pepper to taste and chopped parsley.

Transfer to a heated platter and serve immediately.

NOTE
This is an easy dish to cook at a side table in the dining room.

Nutrition Facts Per Serving: 175 calories, 10 g total fat (3 g saturated), 125 mg cholesterol, 5 g carbohydrate, 16 g protein, 247 mg sodium

18 large prawns (about 1 pound)
2 large cloves garlic, minced
¼ teaspoon salt
2 tablespoons butter
2 tablespoons olive oil
2 tablespoons freshly squeezed
    lemon juice
2 tablespoons white wine
1 cup sliced mushrooms
1 green onion, sliced
1 large ripe tomato, peeled and
    finely diced
Freshly ground pepper to taste
1 tablespoon chopped fresh parsley

Spring Shrimp with Pasta

With such glorious colors, this dish needs no garnish.

Yield: 4 servings

Bring 8 cups salted water to a boil. Cook pasta *al dente*.

While pasta is cooking, sauté garlic in butter in a large frying pan. Add asparagus, peas, and green onions. Cook, stirring, 3 to 4 minutes or until tender yet crisp. Quickly stir in the shrimp, red pepper slices, 2 tablespoons parsley, basil, red pepper flakes, and wine. Cook just to heat through.

To assemble the dish, place the hot, drained pasta on a large heated serving platter; top with the shrimp sauce, grated cheese, seasonings, and remaining 2 tablespoons parsley. Toss just before serving.

Nutrition Facts Per Serving: 388 calories, 7 g total fat (4 g saturated), 179 mg cholesterol, 50 g carbohydrate, 29 g protein, 460 mg sodium

8 ounces dry pasta, such as fettucini
    or angel hair pasta
1½ tablespoons butter
1 clove garlic, minced
¾ cup thinly sliced asparagus
¾ cup tiny peas, thawed if frozen
½ cup thinly sliced green onion
¾ pound cooked salad shrimp
½ cup thinly sliced red bell pepper
4 tablespoons chopped fresh parsley,
    divided
½ teaspoon dried basil
⅛ teaspoon crushed red pepper
    flakes
2 tablespoons white wine
2 tablespoons freshly grated
    Parmesan cheese
¼ teaspoon salt
⅛ teaspoon pepper

Spicy Coastal Clams

Colorful, with a robust flavor…and only minutes to put together.

Yield: 2 entrée or 4 appetizer servings

1 cup white wine
1 cup tomato sauce
1 bay leaf
1 red bell pepper, chopped
2 teaspoons dried basil
½ teaspoon dried thyme
2 teaspoons chopped fresh parsley
1 medium onion, finely chopped
2 cloves garlic, minced
¼ teaspoon cayenne pepper, or to
taste
2 dozen steamer (butter) clams

Sourdough French bread

In a large, shallow pan with a tight-fitting lid, prepare the broth by combining all ingredients except the clams; bring to a boil and cook about 5 minutes.

Add the clams, return to boiling, cover, and cook another 5 minutes, or until the shells open; discard any shells that do not open and remove bay leaf. Serve clams in bowls with some of the broth, accompanied by sourdough French bread for dipping.

NOTE

If you dig the clams yourself, clean them by soaking them for an hour in fresh water to which you have added a handful of cornmeal. This allows clams to clean any sand from their shells.

Nutrition Facts Per Entrée Serving (without bread): 152 calories, 0.8 g total fat (0 g saturated), 6 mg cholesterol, 15 g carbohydrate, 5 g protein, 764 mg sodium

Rosy Scallops and Linguini

Sun-dried tomatoes give the sauce a rosy pink hue and tangy flavor.

Yield: 3 servings

½ cup sun-dried tomatoes packed
in oil
1 clove garlic, minced
1 pound bay scallops
⅓ cup thinly sliced green onions
1½ tablespoons chopped fresh basil
or 1 teaspoon dried
¼ teaspoon white pepper
1 cup chicken broth
¾ cup dry vermouth
1 cup evaporated skim milk or light
cream
8 ounces dry linguini

GARNISH
Fresh basil sprigs
Freshly grated Parmesan cheese

Drain tomatoes and reserve 2 tablespoons tomato oil. Chop the tomatoes; set aside.

In a large frying pan, heat the reserved tomato oil over medium heat; add garlic and scallops, stirring often until scallops are opaque, about 3 minutes. Remove scallops from frying pan.

To the pan, add onions, basil, tomatoes, pepper, broth, and vermouth. Boil over high heat, stirring, until reduced by half.

Reduce heat to low, add milk, and bring to a simmer. Add the reserved scallops and heat through.

Meanwhile, cook pasta according to package directions; drain and arrange on plates. Spoon sauce over pasta; garnish with basil and Parmesan cheese.

Nutrition Facts Per Serving (with skim milk): 403 calories, 11 g total fat (2 g saturated), 54 mg cholesterol, 23 g carbohydrate, 37 g protein, 1,062 mg sodium

Beachcomber's Spaghetti

An elegant way to serve spaghetti…and easy to assemble.

Yield: 4 servings

Drain canned clams reserving juice. In a small bowl, combine ¾ cup reserved clam juice, chicken stock, and wine.

In a medium saucepan, sauté garlic, mushrooms, and onions in oil over medium heat for 5 minutes or until tender. Add flour and mix well. Gradually blend in combined liquids. Bring mixture to a boil, stirring constantly until thickened.

Add canned clams, parsley, oregano, and thyme. Reduce heat and simmer 5 minutes.

Meanwhile, cook spaghetti according to package directions.

While spaghetti is cooking, rinse fresh clams under cold water. Discard any clams that do not close when tapped. In a large saucepan, steam fresh clams in a few inches of water until shells open, about 5 minutes. Discard any shells that do not open during cooking. Set clams aside.

Drain spaghetti and transfer to a large bowl. Pour sauce over pasta and toss well. Divide pasta among individual serving dishes and top with fresh clams. Sprinkle with Parmesan cheese, if desired. Serve immediately.

Nutrition Facts Per Serving: 690 calories, 12 g total fat (1 g saturated), 91 mg cholesterol, 92 g carbohydrate, 52 g protein, 394 mg sodium

2 cans (6.5 ounces each) chopped clams
1 cup chicken stock
¼ cup dry white wine
2 tablespoons vegetable oil
2 cloves garlic, minced
½ cup chopped fresh mushrooms
6 green onions, sliced
2 tablespoons all-purpose flour
¼ cup chopped fresh parsley
½ teaspoon dried oregano
¼ teaspoon dried thyme leaves
12 ounces dry spaghetti
¾ pound fresh clams
Freshly grated Parmesan cheese, optional

Stifatho

Nuts and cheese give this Greek stew an Oregon twist.

Yield: 12 servings

In a large saucepan over medium-high heat, brown the meat in the oil, being careful not to crowd the meat, or it will steam rather than brown.

Add the onion and continue cooking until onion is transparent.

Combine the tomato paste, wine or water, and vinegar. Add to the meat with the garlic and bay leaf; salt and pepper to taste. Cover and simmer 1 hour.

Add the pearl onions; simmer 1 hour. Remove bay leaf.

Stir in the walnuts and cubed cheese. Simmer 5 minutes, or until the cheese melts into the sauce. Serve over rice or noodles.

Nutrition Facts Per Serving (without rice or noodles): 295 calories, 22 g total fat (9 g saturated), 71 mg cholesterol, 6 g carbohydrate, 19 g protein, 382 mg sodium

5 tablespoons olive oil
3 pounds lean beef, cubed
1 medium onion, chopped
1 can (6 ounces) tomato paste
1½ cups red wine or water
2 tablespoons red wine vinegar
1 clove garlic, minced
1 bay leaf
Salt and pepper to taste
2 pounds pearl onions, peeled
¾ cup walnut halves
½ pound Gouda cheese, cubed

MARINATED FLANK STEAK

1½ pounds flank steak
½ cup lemon juice
½ cup soy sauce
½ cup vegetable oil
¼–½ cup prepared mustard

Neighbors may come a-running when the aroma of this grilled steak wafts through the neighborhood.

Yield: 6 servings

Pierce the steak in several places with a sharp fork; place in a shallow dish. In a small bowl, combine lemon juice, soy sauce, and oil; pour over meat. Marinate in refrigerator for 10 hours or up to 2 days, turning several times.

Preheat grill. Drain marinade; spread mustard on one side of steak. Grill 5 to 8 minutes. Turn meat, spread with remaining mustard, and grill as desired.

Carve across the grain into very thin slices.

Nutrition Facts Per Serving: 259 calories, 17 g total fat (6 g saturated), 58 mg cholesterol, 2 g carbohydrate, 23 g protein, 606 mg sodium

BEEF FLAMBÉ

3 tablespoons flour
1 teaspoon salt
1 teaspoon dried oregano
½ teaspoon pepper
2 pounds beef round steak, cut into 1½-inch cubes
4 tablespoons olive oil
½ cup garlic-flavored vinegar
½ cup dry red wine
½ cup beef consommé, undiluted
1 bay leaf
12 white pearl onions, peeled
1 large green pepper, sliced
½ pound mushrooms, sliced
1 cup cherry tomatoes, halved
¼ cup brandy

Present this rich beef stew in a pretty heatproof dish and flame it at the table. Delicious served over rice or noodles.

Yield: 8 servings

Toss steak cubes in flour which has been mixed with the salt, oregano, and pepper.

In a large, heavy skillet or Dutch oven, brown the meat in the oil, turning to brown all sides.

In a small bowl, combine vinegar, wine, consommé, and bay leaf. Add to the meat, stirring as it cooks and thickens. Cover and simmer 1 hour, stirring 2 or 3 times.

Add onions; cook 10 minutes over medium heat.

Add green pepper and mushrooms; cook 5 minutes.

Add tomatoes and cook 5 minutes more. Remove bay leaf. Spoon beef, sauce, and vegetables into a heatproof serving dish. Warm the brandy. At the table, pour the brandy over the meat and flame. When the flame dies, stir gently and serve.

Nutrition Facts Per Serving: 372 calories, 21 g total fat (6 g saturated), 67 mg cholesterol, 14 g carbohydrate, 25 g protein, 1,112 mg sodium

Cascade Beef Casserole

Ginger, curry, and horseradish lend an unusual flavor to the sauce. This would also be great served over a baked potato!

Yield: 8 servings

Preheat oven to 300 degrees.

Spray a large skillet with nonstick spray. Brown the meat cubes; transfer to an oven-proof casserole.

Re-spray the skillet and brown the onion slices. Add onions to the casserole along with the next 6 ingredients (curry through wine).

Cover and bake at 300 degrees for 2½ to 3 hours.

Combine sour cream, horseradish, and chopped parsley. Stir mixture into meat just before serving.

Nutrition Facts Per Serving: 286 calories, 18 g total fat (8 g saturated), 77 mg cholesterol, 3 g carbohydrate, 23 g protein, 305 mg sodium

2 pounds beef round steak cut into 1½-inch cubes
1 large onion, thinly sliced
1 teaspoon curry powder
½ teaspoon ground ginger
1½ tablespoons Worcestershire sauce
½ teaspoon salt
¼ teaspoon pepper
¾ cup white wine
¾ cup sour cream
1 tablespoon horseradish
1 tablespoon chopped fresh parsley

Beef Roulade

These beef rolls are wonderful with "Broccoli-stuffed Onions" on page 109. Single-sized portions make this an excellent buffet entrée choice.

Yield: 6 servings

Preheat oven to 350 degrees.

Combine cornstarch, salt, and pepper on a piece of waxed paper. Set aside.

Heat oil in a skillet; sauté onion until transparent. Drain and remove to a bowl. In the same skillet, cook bacon until limp. Add to the onions.

Cut steak into 6 rectangles of approximately equal size. Divide onion mixture over them. Roll up each piece beginning with the long side; fasten with a toothpick.

Coat each roll with the cornstarch mixture; brown in the same skillet, sprinkling any remaining cornstarch mixture over the meat. Place rolls in an ovenproof casserole.

Combine the catsup, water, and Worcestershire sauce; pour over the meat rolls. Cover and bake for 1 hour or until done.

NOTE
Ask the butcher to cut meat across the grain into ⅛-inch slices.

Nutrition Facts Per Serving: 321 calories, 20 g total fat (6 g saturated), 70 mg cholesterol, 11 g carbohydrate, 23 g protein, 632 mg sodium

5 tablespoons cornstarch
1 teaspoon salt
1 teaspoon pepper
2 tablespoons vegetable oil
½ cup chopped onion
3 slices bacon, chopped
1½ pounds beef round steak, sliced ⅛-inch thick
⅓ cup catsup
½ cup water
1 teaspoon Worcestershire sauce

2 boneless pork loins (1½ pounds each)

MUSTARD-CAPER SAUCE
⅓ cup olive oil
4 tablespoons Dijon mustard
½ teaspoon Worcestershire sauce
½ cup white wine, divided
½ cup half-and-half cream
3–4 tablespoons capers, drained

Pork Roast with Mustard-Caper Sauce

Perfect for company! Its aroma while roasting whets all appetites.

Yield: 12 servings

Preheat oven to 350 degrees.

Blend olive oil, mustard, Worcestershire sauce and ¼ cup of the wine. Spread 1 loin with some of the mustard mixture. Place second loin on top of the first to form a roast. Tie the roast in several places with butcher's string and spread mustard mixture on top of the loins; reserve remaining mustard mixture. Bake, covered, at 350 degrees for 2 hours or until done.

Remove roast from the pan and keep it warm. Deglaze the pan with the remaining ¼ cup wine; add the reserved mustard mix. Just before serving, add the cream and capers; heat through. Slice the roast and serve with sauce.

Nutrition Facts Per Serving: 205 calories, 12 g total fat (3 g saturated), 54 mg cholesterol, 1 g carbohydrate, 20 g protein, 136 mg sodium

1 teaspoon butter
2 medium onions, chopped
1½ pounds boneless pork butt roast, cut into 1-inch cubes
3 cups water
2 tablespoons Hungarian sweet paprika
1½ teaspoons seasoned salt
4 cans (14 ounces each) sauerkraut
1 teaspoon sugar
½ cup sour cream for topping

Paprika Pork

Best when made one or two days ahead.

Yield: 8 servings

In a frying pan, sauté onions in butter until transparent; add pork cubes and brown them on all sides.

Add water, paprika, and salt. Stir over medium-high heat for about 5 minutes. Lower heat; simmer, covered, for 1½ to 2 hours, or until the meat is tender, and the liquid is reduced by ⅓. Stir occasionally.

Meanwhile, rinse sauerkraut with very warm water; drain. Put sauerkraut in a large saucepan and cover with water. Bring to a boil; then lower heat and simmer for 30 minutes. Drain.

Add sauerkraut and sugar to the pork. Cook 15 minutes.

Serve in bowls, each topped with a tablespoon of sour cream.

Nutrition Facts Per Serving: 238 calories, 16 g total fat (6 g saturated), 53 mg cholesterol, 12 g carbohydrate, 14 g protein, 1,093 mg sodium

ERBED LAMB DIJON

Butterflied leg of lamb is grilled over coals and basted with a flavorful marinade. This dish has converted more than a few into lovers of lamb.

Yield: 12 servings

Place the flattened lamb in a shallow pan. Combine the remaining ingredients and pour the marinade over the lamb, coating the meat thoroughly. Cover and marinate at room temperature for about 1 hour. Then refrigerate and marinate an additional 4 hours, turning meat occasionally.

Preheat barbecue coals.

Remove lamb from marinade; pat dry. To hold it flat, place lamb in a grilling rack or thread 3 or 4 skewers through it.

Place lamb over medium-hot coals; cook for 60 to 90 minutes, basting occasionally with marinade. The lamb is best when still slightly pink inside.

In a small saucepan, bring the remaining marinade to a boil and simmer for 3 to 5 minutes. Serve in a separate bowl accompanying the sliced meat.

Nutrition Facts Per Serving: 405 calories, 31 g total fat (12 g saturated), 103 mg cholesterol, 2 g carbohydrate, 28 g protein, 272 mg sodium

5-pound leg of lamb, boned and
    butterflied
½–¾ cup Dijon mustard
½ cup dry white wine
¼ cup vegetable oil
4 cloves garlic, minced
1½ teaspoons crushed dried
    rosemary
1 teaspoon dried basil
½ teaspoon dried oregano
½ teaspoon dried thyme
¼ teaspoon pepper

INE NUT-TURKEY LOAF

Serve with pasta tossed with olive oil, grated lemon peel, and lots of chopped parsley.

Yield: 6 servings

Preheat oven to 375 degrees.

In a large bowl, lightly combine all ingredients. Transfer to an 8x4-inch loaf pan.

Bake 50 minutes, or until loaf pulls away from sides of pan and top is golden brown.

Nutrition Facts Per Serving: 296 calories, 17 g total fat (4 g saturated), 97 mg cholesterol, 19 g carbohydrate, 21 g protein, 326 mg sodium

1 pound ground turkey
1 medium onion, chopped
¾ cup dry bread crumbs
¼ cup quick-cooking rolled oats
⅓ cup Marsala wine, or milk
1 large egg, beaten
½ cup pine nuts, toasted and
    chopped
⅓ cup chopped sun-dried tomatoes
    in oil, drained
1 clove garlic, minced
1 tablespoon chopped fresh
    rosemary or 1 teaspoon dried
1 tablespoon chopped fresh oregano
    or 1 teaspoon dried
1 teaspoon salt
¼ teaspoon pepper

Haystack Rock at Cannon Beach is the world's third largest free-standing monolith. With a backdrop of the Pacific Ocean and spectacular sunsets, it's easily one of the most photogenic sites in the state.

Elegant Eggplant Stacks

A light approach to moussaka—individual stacks of eggplant and lamb filling, flavored with dill and mint.

Yield: 4 servings

1 eggplant, 6–8 inches long
2 tablespoons salt, divided
1 tablespoon olive oil
1 medium onion, diced
1 pound ground lamb
1 teaspoon salt
⅛ teaspoon pepper
1 tablespoon dried dill weed
1 tablespoon chopped fresh mint
    leaves
3 cups quartered fresh Roma
    tomatoes
1 tablespoon chopped fresh parsley
1 tablespoon dry bread crumbs
Additional chopped mint and
    parsley, for garnish

Preheat oven to 375 degrees.

Cut eggplant into twelve ½-inch slices. Sprinkle 1 tablespoon of salt on 3 thicknesses of paper towels. Lay the eggplant slices on the salted towels, top the slices with another tablespoon of salt, and cover with additional layers of paper towels. Let rest for 20 minutes while you prepare the sauce.

In a large saucepan, sauté the onion in the oil until tender. Add lamb and crumble with a wooden spoon. Cook over medium heat until browned. Pour off any fat.

Add salt, pepper, dill weed, mint, and tomatoes; cook over medium heat, stirring occasionally, until the sauce thickens.

Rinse the eggplant slices; pat dry. Place 4 of the larger slices in the bottom of an 8-inch square baking pan. Spoon about ⅓ of the meat sauce over the eggplant; top with 4 more slices. Repeat layers of sauce and eggplant, using all the sauce.

In a small bowl, combine chopped parsley and bread crumbs; sprinkle over the stacks. Cover the dish and bake at 375 degrees for 1 hour. Remove the cover and bake 10 minutes longer.

Serve with additional chopped mint and parsley sprinkled over the top.

Nutrition Facts Per Serving: 421 calories, 31 g total fat (12 g saturated), 83 mg cholesterol, 16 g carbohydrate, 22 g protein, 760 mg sodium

Eggplant Pizzas

Perfect for snacks or a main dish.

Yield: 4 servings

1 medium eggplant
1 large egg, beaten
½ cup dry bread crumbs
⅓ cup vegetable oil
¼ cup grated Parmesan cheese
1 teaspoon dried oregano
¼ pound sliced salami
12 ounces spaghetti sauce
¼ pound mozzarella cheese, sliced

Preheat oven to 350 degrees. Spray a baking sheet with a nonstick spray.

Peel eggplant; cut into ¼-inch round slices.

Dip eggplant slices in beaten egg and then coat with bread crumbs. Brown eggplant slices in large frying pan with oil.

Place browned slices on prepared baking sheet; sprinkle with grated Parmesan cheese and oregano. Top each piece with a slice of salami, dot with 1 tablespoon spaghetti sauce, and cover with a slice of mozzarella cheese.

Bake for 5 to 10 minutes at 350 degrees, or until cheese is melted.

Nutrition Facts Per Serving: 542 calories, 39 g total fat (11 g saturated), 101 mg cholesterol, 32 g carbohydrate, 18 g protein, 1,206 mg sodium

Bow Tie Pasta with Garlic-Vermouth Sauce

Robust flavor and easy preparation make this pasta dish a winner.

Yield: 4 servings

In a large pot, bring 3 quarts salted water to a rolling boil. Add pasta and cook *al dente*, about 10 to 13 minutes. Drain pasta and coat with 2 tablespoons olive oil.

Meanwhile, heat 6 tablespoons olive oil in a large frying pan; add garlic and shallots. Sauté until vegetables are lightly browned.

Add tomatoes, parsley, cilantro, mushrooms, if used, and vermouth. Cook over medium heat until liquid is reduced by half.

Add pasta to sauce. Season to taste with salt and pepper. Heat thoroughly but do not overcook. Serve in warmed pasta bowls and top pasta with pine nuts, capers, green onions, and Parmesan cheese.

Nutrition Facts Per Serving: 548 calories, 29 g total fat (4 g saturated), 0 mg cholesterol, 57 g carbohydrate, 10 g protein, 50 mg sodium

8 ounces bow tie pasta
8 tablespoons olive oil, divided
5 large cloves garlic, minced
3 large shallots, minced
5 Roma tomatoes, seeded and diced
2 tablespoons chopped fresh parsley
1 tablespoon chopped fresh cilantro
Sliced shitake mushrooms, optional
½ cup extra-dry vermouth
Salt and pepper to taste

GARNISH
Pine nuts
Capers
Green onion tops, finely julienned
Freshly grated Parmesan cheese

Spaghetti Verdi

A parsley pesto that stays bright and fresh.

Yield: 6 servings

Prepare Parsley Pesto by processing ingredients in blender or food processor until they are puréed.

In a large pot of boiling salted water, cook pasta *al dente*.

Drain the pasta and turn into a large serving bowl. Toss with the sauce, butter, walnuts, and cheese. Serve immediately.

Nutrition Facts Per Serving: 625 calories, 32 g total fat (7 g saturated), 15 mg cholesterol, 69 g carbohydrate, 20 g protein, 614 mg sodium

1 pound dry spaghetti
2 tablespoons butter
½ cup chopped walnuts
½ cup freshly grated Parmesan
     cheese

PARSLEY PESTO
2 cups fresh parsley, stems removed
1 tablespoon fresh basil or
     1 teaspoon dried
1 tablespoon fresh oregano or
     1 teaspoon dried
1 tablespoon fresh marjoram or
     1 teaspoon dried
1 clove garlic
1 teaspoon salt
½ teaspoon pepper
½ cup olive oil

1½ cups dry black beans
8 cups water, divided
1 clove garlic, minced
1 teaspoon salt
½ teaspoon cumin
Dash of hot pepper sauce
1 tablespoon vegetable oil
1 cup chopped onion
1 cup chopped green pepper
2 cups long grain rice

FRESH SALSA
1 large ripe tomato, chopped
¾ cup diced onion
1 tablespoon cider vinegar
1 teaspoon vegetable oil
3 drops of hot pepper sauce

$\mathscr{S}$avory Black Beans and Rice

You don't have to be vegetarian to appreciate this flavorful combination.

Yield: 8 servings

Sort and wash the beans. In a large pot, soak the beans overnight in 4 cups water or use quick-soak method (see "Navy Bean and Chicken Soup," page 50).

Drain beans and return them to the pot with 4 cups fresh water. Bring to a boil; add the garlic, salt, cumin, and hot pepper sauce. Reduce heat and cook until the beans are tender, about 2 hours.

In a medium frying pan, sauté the onion and green pepper in the oil. Stir into the cooked beans.

Cook the rice according to package directions and keep hot.

Combine all salsa ingredients in a medium bowl.

Serve the beans over hot rice topped with fresh salsa.

Nutrition Facts Per Serving: 285 calories, 3 g total fat (0 g saturated), 0 mg cholesterol, 57 g carbohydrate, 9 g protein, 341 mg sodium

1 medium eggplant
2–4 tablespoons olive oil
1 cup chopped yellow onion
1 cup chopped celery
1 cup chopped green pepper
4 cloves garlic, minced
1½ pounds fresh Roma tomatoes,
    peeled and chopped
2 tablespoons chili powder
1 tablespoon ground cumin
1 tablespoon dried oregano
1 tablespoon dried basil
2 teaspoons pepper
1 teaspoon salt
¼ cup chopped fresh parsley
1 can (15 ounces) each, kidney,
    chili, and red beans, drained
2 tablespoons cider vinegar

$\mathscr{V}$egetarian Chili

Serve with brown rice for a wholesome meatless meal.

Yield: 8 servings

Cut unpeeled eggplant into ½-inch cubes. Place in colander; sprinkle with salt. Let stand 1 hour; drain eggplant on paper towels and pat dry.

In a large frying pan, sauté the eggplant in olive oil until almost tender. Remove eggplant to a large soup pot using a slotted spoon.

In the same frying pan, sauté onion, celery, green pepper, and garlic about 10 minutes, adding more oil if necessary. Remove to the soup pot.

Add the tomatoes and seasonings to the pot. Cook 30 minutes over medium heat.

Add the 3 kinds of beans; bring to simmer. Stir in vinegar and serve over brown rice.

NOTE
One can (35 ounces) Italian plum tomatoes, chopped, can be used instead of the fresh Roma tomatoes.

Nutrition Facts Per Serving: 219 calories, 6 g total fat (0.6 g saturated), 0 mg cholesterol, 37 g carbohydrate, 11 g protein, 1,022 mg sodium

Side Dishes

2 pounds fresh asparagus, tough
    ends removed

SESAME-GINGER SAUCE
3 tablespoons soy sauce
3 tablespoons white wine vinegar
¼ cup toasted sesame seeds
2 large cloves garlic, peeled and
    finely minced
2 teaspoons finely minced fresh
    ginger root
¼ teaspoon prepared Chinese
    mustard
3 tablespoons vegetable oil
3 tablespoons sesame oil

SESAME-GINGER ASPARAGUS

Enhance asparagus with a hint of intrigue.

Yield: 8 servings

Cook asparagus, covered, in a large pan of simmering water for 3 to 5 minutes or until tender yet crisp.

Whisk together the soy sauce, vinegar, sesame seeds, garlic, ginger root, and mustard. Whisk in the vegetable and sesame oils. Drizzle over hot or chilled asparagus.

NOTE
Sesame-Ginger Sauce may be prepared several days in advance.

Nutrition Facts Per Serving: 127 calories, 13 g total fat (2 g saturated), 0 mg cholesterol, 2 g carbohydrate, 2 g protein, 315 mg sodium

---

2 pounds fresh asparagus, tough
    ends removed

PEPPERCORN SAUCE
2 tablespoons mayonnaise
2 tablespoons white wine vinegar
½ teaspoon Worcestershire sauce
3 tablespoons extra-virgin olive oil
1 tablespoon green peppercorns,
    drained, rinsed, and chopped
½ medium red pepper, roasted,
    peeled, and finely chopped
Salt to taste
Freshly ground pepper to taste

ASPARAGUS WITH PEPPERCORNS

A peppy sauce adds a lively bite to asparagus.

Yield: 8 servings

Cook asparagus according to previous recipe.

To make Peppercorn Sauce, whisk together the mayonnaise, vinegar, and Worcestershire sauce. Whisk in the olive oil in a slow and steady stream. Stir in the chopped peppercorns, red pepper, salt, and pepper. Refrigerate 1 to 24 hours.

Bring sauce to room temperature and serve over hot or chilled asparagus.

Nutrition Facts Per Serving: 77 calories, 8 g total fat (1 g saturated), 2 mg cholesterol, 2 g carbohydrate, 1 g protein, 24 mg sodium

---

¾ cup firmly packed brown sugar
½ cup catsup
⅓ cup dark corn syrup
2–3 teaspoons liquid smoke
    flavoring
2 teaspoons Dijon mustard
3 drops hot pepper sauce
1 medium onion, diced
4 strips bacon, diced and cooked
4 cans (15 ounces each) butter
    beans, drained

BARBECUED BUTTER BEANS

Try a different bean to bake!

Yield: 8 servings

Preheat oven to 325 degrees. Combine all the ingredients and mix well. Turn into a 1½-quart casserole.

Bake uncovered for 1 hour.

Nutrition Facts Per Serving: 437 calories, 3 g total fat (0.6 g saturated), 3 mg cholesterol, 85 g carbohydrate, 23 g protein, 400 mg sodium

Broccoli with Creamy Mustard Sauce

This sauce also works well on asparagus or as dip for artichoke leaves.

Yield: 6 servings

Steam broccoli until tender yet crisp, approximately 8 to 12 minutes.

Toast almonds until golden.

Meanwhile, make Creamy Mustard Sauce. In a small saucepan over medium heat, melt butter; stir in flour and heat until foamy. Add sour cream, mayonnaise, and mustard, stirring constantly until heated through. Do not boil.

Arrange broccoli on a serving platter. Pour the sauce over broccoli; sprinkle with toasted almonds.

Nutrition Facts Per Serving: 173 calories, 17 g total fat (5 g saturated), 19 mg cholesterol, 5 g carbohydrate, 3 g protein, 122 mg sodium

2 pounds fresh broccoli spears
4 tablespoons slivered almonds

CREAMY MUSTARD SAUCE
1 tablespoon butter
1 tablespoon flour
½ cup sour cream
¼ cup mayonnaise
1 tablespoon prepared mustard

Far-East Broccoli

Adding a lively sauce lifts broccoli to new heights.

Yield: 4 servings

Steam broccoli until tender yet crisp, approximately 4 to 8 minutes.

In a small bowl, combine vinegar, sesame oil, soy sauce, and mustard. Pour over the broccoli and toss to coat. May be served hot or cold.

Nutrition Facts Per Serving: 89 calories, 7 g total fat (1 g saturated), 0 mg cholesterol, 5 g carbohydrate, 3 g protein, 193 mg sodium

4 cups broccoli florets
1 tablespoon rice wine vinegar
2 tablespoons sesame oil
2 teaspoons soy sauce
2 teaspoons prepared mustard

Brussels Sprouts Vinaigrette

A hot vinaigrette dressing flavors this often overlooked vegetable.

Yield: 6 servings

In large saucepan, cook Brussels sprouts in an inch of water until tender; drain.

Cook bacon in a small frying pan until crisp. Remove the bacon and pour off almost all the fat. Add the chopped onion; cook until transparent. Add vinegar, honey, mustard, and bacon; stir to blend. Pour over sprouts, toss, and serve immediately.

Nutrition Facts Per Serving: 86 calories, 2 g total fat (0.8 g saturated), 4 mg cholesterol, 15 g carbohydrate, 4 g protein, 139 mg sodium

4 cups fresh Brussels sprouts, or 20 ounces frozen
4 strips bacon, diced
½ medium onion, chopped
3 tablespoons cider vinegar
3 tablespoons honey
1 teaspoon prepared mustard

1 medium head red cabbage, thinly
sliced
4–5 tablespoons red wine vinegar
1 tablespoon butter
1 medium onion, thinly sliced
2 medium, unpeeled tart apples,
finely diced
2 tablespoons sugar
1 tablespoon all-purpose flour
1 teaspoon salt
¼ teaspoon pepper
¼ cup apple juice or water

BAKED RED CABBAGE

This mellow sweet-and-sour cabbage is perfect for fall dinners.

Yield: 8 servings

Preheat oven to 325 degrees. Grease a 9x13-inch baking dish.

In a large saucepan, cook the cabbage in boiling water for 2 to 3 minutes; drain. Sprinkle with vinegar and toss to coat. The color of the cabbage will change.

In a large frying pan, sauté the onion in butter for 1 minute. Add the apples and continue cooking for 3 to 4 minutes, until apples are soft.

In a small bowl, combine sugar, flour, and seasonings. Add this to cabbage along with the onion mixture. Stir in apple juice or water.

Spoon mixture into the prepared baking dish. Cover and bake at 325 degrees for 1½ hours, or until cabbage is tender.

Nutrition Facts Per Serving: 88 calories, 2 g total fat (1 g saturated), 4 mg cholesterol, 18 g carbohydrate, 2 g protein, 362 mg sodium

1 tablespoon olive oil
3 tablespoons butter, divided
2 large cloves garlic, minced
1 small head red cabbage, thinly
shredded
Freshly ground pepper
6 medium potatoes, peeled and
quartered
⅓ cup milk
Salt to taste
2 cups grated sharp Cheddar cheese
2 ounces feta cheese, crumbled
Paprika

CABBAGE COMBO

Lively variation of a hearty potato favorite.

Yield: 8 servings

Preheat oven to 350 degrees. Grease a 9x13-inch baking dish.

In a large frying pan, sauté the garlic in olive oil and 1 tablespoon butter until fragrant. Add shredded cabbage and sauté until wilted but not soft. Season with a generous amount of pepper; set aside.

In a large saucepan, boil potatoes in salted water until tender; drain. Mash potatoes with milk, 2 tablespoons butter, and salt to taste.

Spread potatoes in the prepared baking dish. Cover with the sautéed cabbage.

Bake at 350 degrees for 15 minutes or until hot. Remove from oven and top with the cheeses and sprinkle with paprika. Return to oven for 10 minutes, or until cheeses melt and are lightly browned.

Nutrition Facts Per Serving: 329 calories, 18 g total fat (10 g saturated), 49 mg cholesterol, 23 g carbohydrate, 12 g protein, 321 mg sodium

CARROT-APPLE CASSEROLE

A colorful side dish that combines a healthful vegetable with three tasty fruits.

Yield: 8 servings

Preheat oven to 350 degrees.

In a large mixing bowl, combine the apples, carrots, and dried cranberries.

Mix together the flour and sugar. Toss with the apples, carrots, and cranberries, coating well.

Turn into a 2½-quart casserole. Dot with butter. Pour orange juice over all.

Cover and bake at 350 degrees for 1 hour.

Nutrition Facts Per Serving: 184 calories, 6 g total fat (4 g saturated), 15 mg cholesterol, 33 g carbohydrate, 1 g protein, 78 mg sodium

5 medium apples, peeled and thinly sliced
1 pound carrots, peeled and thinly sliced
¼ cup dried cranberries
3 tablespoons all-purpose flour
5 tablespoons sugar
¼ cup butter
¾ cup fresh orange juice

CAULIFLOWER WITH SWISS CHEESE SAUCE

Lovely for a holiday table, with its red-and-green flecked sauce!

Yield: 8 servings

Preheat oven to 325 degrees.

Break cauliflower into florets. Cook in a small amount of boiling water until tender yet crisp, about 8 minutes; drain.

Meanwhile, prepare the Swiss Cheese Sauce. In a medium saucepan, sauté mushrooms and green pepper in butter until tender. Blend in the flour; whisk in the milk. Cook, stirring constantly, over medium heat until thickened. Stir in salt, cheese, and pimientos. Remove from heat.

Generously grease a 2-quart casserole. Place half the cauliflower in the prepared casserole; cover with half the sauce. Add the remaining cauliflower and top with the remaining sauce.

Bake at 325 degrees for 15 minutes.

Nutrition Facts Per Serving: 169 calories, 12 g total fat (7 g saturated), 37 mg cholesterol, 9 g carbohydrate, 7 g protein, 396 mg sodium

1 large head cauliflower

SWISS CHEESE SAUCE
¼ cup butter
1 cup sliced mushrooms
1 cup diced green pepper
⅓ cup flour
2 cups milk
1 teaspoon salt
1 cup grated Swiss cheese
2 tablespoons diced pimientos

3 large eggs, beaten
½ teaspoon Worcestershire sauce
1 cup low-fat sour cream
1 can (8.7 ounces) cream-style corn
1 can (8.7 ounces) whole-kernel
  corn
½ cup cornmeal
1 can (4 ounces) chopped green
  chilies
6 ounces Monterey Jack cheese,
  diced
6 ounces sharp Cheddar cheese,
  diced

CHILI-CHEESE CORN PIE

A quick "toss-together" for busy cooks—serves as a side dish or an entrée.

Yield: 8 servings

Preheat oven to 350 degrees. Grease a 10-inch quiche or pie pan.

In a medium bowl, combine beaten eggs, Worcestershire sauce, and sour cream.

Add both cans of corn and cornmeal; stir in chilies. Pour into prepared pan.

Top with both cheeses, distributing evenly.

Bake at 350 degrees for 1 hour; allow pie to rest 5 minutes before serving.

Nutrition Facts Per Serving: 349 calories, 22 g total fat (12 g saturated), 20 mg cholesterol, 19 g carbohydrate, 20 g protein, 490 mg sodium

¼ cup butter
2 cups corn, fresh or frozen
½ cup chopped green pepper
½ cup chopped pimientos
½ cup sliced green olives
¼ cup chopped fresh parsley
¼ cup all-purpose flour
1 teaspoon salt
1 teaspoon pepper
2 cups 1 percent milk
3 large eggs
1 cup grated Cheddar cheese

FIESTA CORN CUSTARD

This tasty custard is filled with colorful vegetables.

Yield: 8 servings

Preheat oven to 350 degrees. Lightly grease a 2-quart casserole.

In a large frying pan, melt butter. Add corn, green pepper, pimientos, olives, and parsley. Sauté for 2 minutes; cover and cook over medium heat 10 minutes.

Blend together the flour, salt, and pepper; sprinkle this over the vegetables in pan. Gradually add milk, stirring constantly until mixture is thickened. Remove from heat.

In a large bowl, beat eggs. Gradually stir vegetable mixture into the eggs; do not add all at once or the eggs will scramble. Blend in the cheese.

Turn into prepared casserole. Set casserole in large pan filled to 1-inch depth with hot water. Bake at 350 degrees for 25 to 30 minutes, or until the custard is set and a knife inserted into center comes out clean. Let rest a few minutes before serving.

Nutrition Facts Per Serving: 346 calories, 16 g total fat (8 g saturated), 112 mg cholesterol, 40 g carbohydrate, 13 g protein, 564 mg sodium

Oregon is the largest producer of winter pears in the United States. These golden treasures grow in particular abundance down south in the Rogue River Valley.

Broccoli-Stuffed Onions

Make this attractive dish in advance and bake it just before serving.

Yield: 8 servings

Preheat oven to 350 degrees. Lightly grease a 9-inch square baking pan.

Peel onions and cut in half horizontally. Steam the onion halves 10 minutes, drain, and cool.

Remove centers of onions leaving ¾-inch outer walls. Place shells in prepared baking pan. Chop centers; reserve 1 cup and set aside remainder for another use.

Steam broccoli for 5 minutes; drain.

In a large bowl, combine broccoli, 1 cup chopped onion centers, cheese, mayonnaise, lemon juice, and garlic.

Distribute the broccoli mixture among onion shells. Cover and refrigerate if preparing in advance.

Bake uncovered at 350 degrees for 20 minutes (30 minutes if refrigerated).

Nutrition Facts Per Serving: 122 calories, 9 g total fat (2 g saturated), 9 mg cholesterol, 7 g carbohydrate, 5 g protein, 163 mg sodium

4 Walla Walla sweet onions or other sweet onions
3 cups chopped broccoli florets
½ cup grated Parmesan cheese
⅓ cup mayonnaise
2 teaspoons freshly squeezed lemon juice
1 clove garlic, peeled and crushed

Crusty-Topped Onions

A fragrant onion dish perfected by its topping.

Yield: 6 servings

Preheat oven to 350 degrees. Lightly grease a shallow 10-inch round baking dish.

Peel and slice onions. Arrange in the prepared baking dish.

Sprinkle thyme, salt, and pepper over the onions and add beef stock. Dot with 1 tablespoon butter.

Cover and bake at 350 degrees for 1½ hours. The onions should become very limp and fragrant.

In a medium bowl, toss cracker crumbs, 2 tablespoons melted butter, and grated cheese. Spread over the onions and bake, uncovered, another 20 to 30 minutes, until the crumbs are browned and some of stock has cooked away.

Nutrition Facts Per Serving: 251 calories, 14 g total fat (7 g saturated), 30 mg cholesterol, 25 g carbohydrate, 7 g protein, 1,176 mg sodium

3 large white onions
¼ teaspoon dried thyme
½ teaspoon salt
¼ teaspoon pepper
1 cup beef stock
1 tablespoon butter
¾ cup butter-cracker crumbs
2 tablespoons butter, melted
¾ cup grated sharp Cheddar cheese

GARDEN PEAS WITH LETTUCE

A microwave version of a French classic.

Yield: 4 servings

2 cups fresh or frozen peas
⅓ cup thinly sliced celery
2 tablespoons water
3 cups shredded iceberg lettuce
1 tablespoon butter, melted
1 tablespoon all-purpose flour
½ teaspoon sugar
¼ cup half-and-half cream

In a 3-quart casserole, combine peas, celery, and water. Cover and microwave on full power for 5 to 7 minutes or until tender.

Stir in the lettuce, cover, and microwave for 2 more minutes, stirring after 1 minute. Lettuce will wilt during cooking. Set mixture aside.

In a small dish, combine butter, flour, and sugar. Blend in cream. Cover and microwave on full power for 1 to 2 minutes, until sauce is thickened. Stir once or twice during cooking.

Drain vegetables. Add sauce to vegetables, tossing to coat. Serve immediately.

Nutrition Facts Per Serving: 111 calories, 5 g total fat (3 g saturated), 13 mg cholesterol, 13 g carbohydrate, 5 g protein, 127 mg sodium

NEW POTATOES IN TARRAGON SAUCE

New potatoes cooked in an herb-scented wine broth—delicious and low-fat.

Yield: 6 servings

2 pounds tiny new potatoes, red or white
1 cup dry vermouth or white wine
1 cup water
⅓ cup tarragon vinegar
1 teaspoon minced garlic
1 tablespoon chopped chives
1 tablespoon minced fresh tarragon or 1 teaspoon dried
¼ cup chopped fresh parsley
2 tablespoons butter
Salt and pepper to taste

Preheat oven to 200 degrees. Grease a 2-quart casserole.

Scrub potatoes but do not peel. Place in a medium saucepan with the wine, water, vinegar, garlic, and chives. Bring to a boil, cover, and reduce heat; simmer until potatoes are tender, about 20 minutes.

Lift potatoes out of the pan and transfer them to the prepared casserole; keep potatoes warm in the oven while sauce is finished. Over high heat, boil the cooking broth until it is reduced by one-third. Stir in the tarragon, parsley, and butter.

Pour the sauce over the potatoes, toss to coat, season to taste, and serve.

Nutrition Facts Per Serving: 102 calories, 4 g total fat (2 g saturated), 10 mg cholesterol, 10 g carbohydrate, 2 g protein, 156 mg sodium

OOT SOUFFLÉ

Autumn vegetables soar to new heights enriched with cheese and toasted walnuts.

Yield: 6 servings

Preheat oven to 350 degrees. Grease a 2½-quart casserole.

Slice the potatoes, parsnips, and carrot into uniform pieces. Place in a large saucepan with water; cover and simmer 20 minutes or until tender.

Drain the vegetables; mash. Blend the egg and milk. Combine mashed vegetables with egg mixture. Salt and pepper to taste; stir in the Cheddar cheese, walnuts, and blue cheese. Spoon into the prepared casserole.

To prepare the topping, sauté the onion in a medium frying pan in olive oil and butter until caramelized; sprinkle with the ground coriander. Add the celery and vinegar; cover, and simmer 7 minutes. Spread over mashed vegetable mixture.

Bake at 350 degrees for 30 to 40 minutes.

Nutrition Facts Per Serving: 273 calories, 16 g total fat (7 g saturated), 66 mg cholesterol, 23 g carbohydrate, 11 g protein, 379 mg sodium

3 medium red potatoes, peeled
2 parsnips, peeled
1 carrot, peeled
1 large egg, beaten
¼ cup milk
Salt and pepper to taste
3 ounces Cheddar cheese, grated
⅓ cup chopped, toasted walnuts
2 ounces Oregon blue cheese or
    other blue cheese, crumbled

TOPPING
1 teaspoon olive oil
1½ tablespoons butter
1 medium onion, sliced
¼ teaspoon ground coriander
2 stalks celery, chopped
2 teaspoons white vinegar

AYERED SPINACH AND ARTICHOKES

An unusual yet elegant combination.

Yield: 8 servings

Preheat oven to 375 degrees.

Drain artichoke hearts; chop and arrange in an ungreased 7x11-inch baking dish. Reserve marinade for another use.

Drain and squeeze dry the spinach. Spread evenly over the artichokes.

In a medium bowl, beat together the cream cheese, butter, and milk. Spread over the vegetable mixture. Sprinkle with pepper and Parmesan cheese.

Cover and bake at 375 degrees for 30 minutes. Uncover and bake 10 minutes or until nicely browned.

Nutrition Facts Per Serving: 301 calories, 25 g total fat (8 g saturated), 33 mg cholesterol, 8 g carbohydrate, 9 g protein, 547 mg sodium

2 jars (6 ounces each) marinated
    artichoke hearts
3 packages (10 ounces each) frozen,
    chopped spinach, thawed
11 ounces low-fat cream cheese,
    softened
2 tablespoons butter, softened
¼ cup milk
Dash of pepper
⅓ cup grated Parmesan cheese

SWEET STEWED TOMATOES

3–4 large tomatoes, peeled and
    chopped
1 large onion, chopped
2 tablespoons cider vinegar
1 teaspoon balsamic vinegar
⅓ cup sugar
¾ teaspoon salt
Pepper to taste
1 tablespoon butter

Dress up an old favorite!

Yield: 4 servings

In a medium saucepan, combine all ingredients. Cover and simmer for 10 minutes, or until onions are tender.

Remove cover and simmer an additional 50 minutes, or until mixture thickens, stirring occasionally to prevent sticking. Serve in small bowls.

Nutrition Facts Per Serving: 124 calories, 3 g total fat (2 g saturated), 8 mg cholesterol, 24 g carbohydrate, 1 g protein, 572 mg sodium

VEGGIE CONFETTI

1 tablespoon butter
2 cups coarsely grated carrots
2 cups coarsely grated parsnips
2 cups coarsely grated, unpeeled
    zucchini
1 tablespoon water
1 teaspoon grated fresh lemon peel,
    optional
Salt and pepper to taste

A simple assembly of fall vegetables, rich in color, not calories.

Yield: 6 servings

In a large frying pan, melt butter. Add prepared vegetables, water, and lemon peel.

Cover and steam over medium-high heat for 2 to 3 minutes. Season with salt and pepper to taste; serve.

NOTE
The coarse grating disc on a food processor works well in this preparation.

Nutrition Facts Per Serving: 66 calories, 2 g total fat (1 g saturated), 5 mg cholesterol, 12 g carbohydrate, 1 g protein, 37 mg sodium

FRYPAN ZUCCHINI

2 tablespoons butter
4 unpeeled zucchini, thinly sliced
    (about 6 cups)
2 tomatoes, peeled and sliced
1 large Walla Walla onion or other
    sweet onion, sliced into rings
1 teaspoon dried sweet basil
Salt and pepper to taste
1 cup grated sharp Cheddar cheese

Tasty, casual fare that combines some of summer's best vegetables.

Yield: 6 servings

Melt butter in a large frying pan.

Place zucchini in the pan and top with sliced tomatoes. Arrange onion rings over tomatoes; sprinkle with basil and salt and pepper to taste.

Cover and cook on medium heat, without stirring, until vegetables are tender. Sprinkle with cheese and serve from the frying pan.

Nutrition Facts Per Serving: 142 calories, 10 g total fat, (6 g saturated), 30 mg cholesterol, 7 g carbohydrate, 7 g protein, 166 mg sodium

Microwave Zucchini Bake

Another delectable use for the prolific zucchini.

Yield: 6 servings

Place zucchini and butter in a 2½-quart ring microwave dish. Cover and microwave for 5 minutes on full power.

Uncover dish and stir in grated cheese, seasonings, and eggs. Sprinkle French-fried onions on top.

Microwave, uncovered, on 50 percent power for 5 minutes. Rotate casserole a quarter turn and microwave another 5 minutes on 50 percent power, or until a knife inserted near center comes out clean.

Nutrition Facts Per Serving: 250 calories, 20 g total fat (10 g saturated), 106 mg cholesterol, 9 g carbohydrate, 8 g protein, 577 mg sodium

1½ pounds unpeeled zucchini, cubed
3 tablespoons butter
1 cup grated Cheddar cheese
¾ teaspoon salt
¼ teaspoon pepper
2 large eggs, beaten
1 can (2.8 ounces) French-fried onions

Triple-Treated Zucchini

Vegetable-stuffed zucchini with a creamy sauce and crumb topping.

Yield: 6 servings

Preheat oven to 350 degrees. Lightly grease a 9x13-inch baking dish.

Slice zucchini lengthwise in half and scoop out centers. Chop the centers coarsely.

In a large frying pan, sauté onion, mushrooms, and chopped zucchini for 3 to 5 minutes. Stir in the bread cubes, corn, and ground nuts. Remove from heat.

Place the zucchini halves in the prepared baking dish and spoon the bread-and-vegetable mixture into hollowed-out centers.

In a small bowl, combine the sour cream, milk, and seasonings. Pour over the tops of the stuffed zucchini halves.

In another small bowl, combine the first 3 topping ingredients. Crumble over the tops of the zucchini. Sprinkle with paprika.

Bake at 350 degrees for 40 to 50 minutes.

NOTE
Chestnuts or pumpkin seeds can be ground easily in a food processor or blender.

Nutrition Facts Per Serving: 463 calories, 25 g total fat (14 g saturated), 52 mg cholesterol, 49 g carbohydrate, 12 g protein, 765 mg sodium

3 medium zucchini
1 onion, diced
½ cup chopped fresh mushrooms
¾ cup soft bread cubes
1 cup corn, fresh or frozen
½ cup roasted chestnuts or toasted pumpkin seeds, ground

SAUCE
1 pint sour cream
½ cup milk
½ teaspoon dried oregano
½ teaspoon salt
¼ teaspoon pepper

TOPPING
½ cup grated Parmesan cheese
¼ cup dry bread crumbs
2 tablespoons butter, melted
Dash of paprika

1½ cups water
1½ teaspoons butter
1 cup instant white rice
1 cup instant brown rice
¼ cup chopped onion
¼ cup chopped red sweet pepper
1 cup diced zucchini
½ cup diced cooked chicken
¼ teaspoon pepper
1 teaspoon garlic powder
¼ cup low-sodium soy sauce

HARLEQUIN RICE

Additional ingredients such as grated carrots, slivered almonds, or green olives can further enhance this microwave dish. Side dish or entrée—you decide.

Yield: 8 servings

In a medium saucepan, bring water and butter to a boil. Stir in the rices and return to a boil. Cover, reduce heat, and simmer 3 minutes. Remove from heat and let stand, covered, 5 minutes. Fluff with a fork.

In a microwave-safe bowl, combine the chopped vegetables and chicken. Microwave on full power for 3 minutes, stirring occasionally.

In a large bowl, toss rices with vegetable mixture, seasonings, and soy sauce. Serve hot.

NOTE
This recipe can also be served cold and garnished with olives.

Nutrition Facts Per Serving: 214 calories, 3 g total fat (2 g saturated), 13 mg cholesterol, 38 g carbohydrate, 7 g protein, 465 mg sodium

1¾ cups water
⅓ cup whole wheat berries
¼ cup brown rice
½ cup barley
½ teaspoon salt
1 cup shredded mozzarella cheese
½ cup cashew nuts, chopped
½ cup raisins
2 cups broccoli florets
1 small yellow pepper, diced
1 medium onion, chopped
1 can (8 ounces) tomato sauce
¼ cup chicken broth
½ teaspoon ground cumin
½ teaspoon ground cinnamon
½ teaspoon ground cardamom
¼ teaspoon crushed red pepper
1 large tomato, chopped

MULTIGRAIN PILAF

Sweet and hot spices distinguish this chewy side dish.

Yield: 8 servings

In a medium saucepan, combine water, wheat berries, brown rice, barley, and salt. Bring to a boil; reduce heat, cover, and simmer 30 minutes. Remove from heat; let stand 10 minutes, covered.

While the grains are still hot, stir in cheese, nuts, and raisins.

In another medium saucepan, combine broccoli, pepper, and onion with a small amount of water. Cook, covered, 2 to 3 minutes. Drain.

Preheat oven to 350 degrees. Lightly grease a 2-quart baking dish.

Spoon the grain mixture into prepared dish. Top with broccoli mixture.

In a small bowl, combine tomato sauce, broth, and spices. Pour over the grains and broccoli. Cover and bake at 350 degrees for 40 minutes.

Top with chopped tomato; cover, let stand 5 to 10 minutes before serving.

Nutrition Facts Per Serving: 243 calories, 8 g total fat (3 g saturated), 13 mg cholesterol, 36 g carbohydrate, 10 g protein, 509 mg sodium

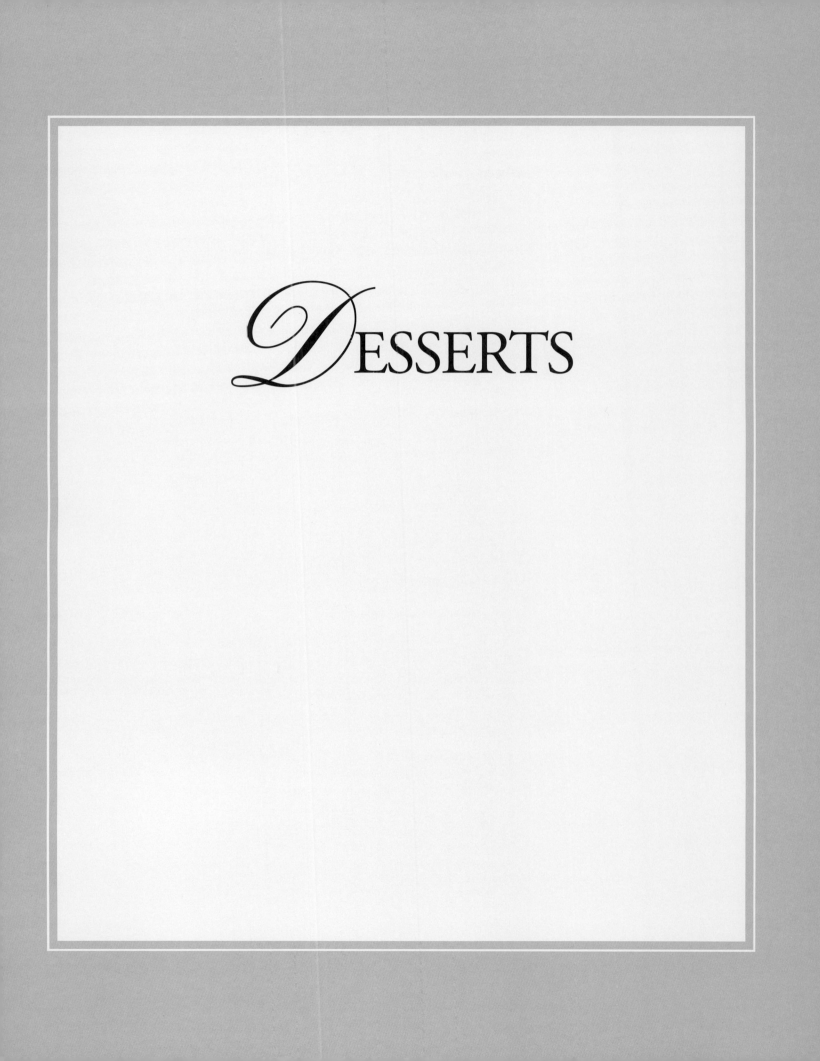

Desserts

32 caramels
5 teaspoons milk
1 cup all-purpose flour
1 cup quick-cooking rolled oats
¾ cup firmly packed brown sugar
½ teaspoon baking soda
½ teaspoon salt
½ cup butter, melted
6 ounces semisweet chocolate chips
½ cup chopped pecans

Country Roads

No better cookie to take on an outing down Oregon's country roads!

Yield: 48 one-inch squares

Preheat oven to 350 degrees. Grease a 7x11-inch pan.

Melt caramels and milk in the top of a double boiler over boiling water; cool melted mixture slightly.

In a large bowl, combine flour, oats, brown sugar, baking soda, salt, and butter with a fork until crumbly. Press half of the mixture in bottom of prepared pan.

Bake at 350 degrees for 10 minutes.

Remove pan from oven and sprinkle baked crust with chocolate chips and pecans. Spread melted caramels over the top and sprinkle with remaining oat mixture.

Bake 15 to 20 minutes or until golden brown. Cool 1 to 2 hours at room temperature before cutting into squares.

Nutrition Facts Per Square: 91 calories, 4 g total fat (2 g saturated), 6 mg cholesterol, 13 g carbohydrate, 1 g protein, 59 mg sodium

2 large egg whites, room
    temperature
¼ teaspoon cream of tartar
⅔ cup sugar
6 ounces white chocolate chips
1 cup chopped nuts
1 teaspoon raspberry liqueur
½ teaspoon raspberry flavoring
4–8 drops red food coloring

Pink Clouds

Light, airy, and full of raspberry flavor.

Yield: 48 one-inch cookies

Preheat oven to 350 degrees. Line 2 large baking sheets with aluminum foil.

Beat egg whites and cream of tartar with mixer until soft peaks form. Gradually add sugar, 1 tablespoon at a time, while beating constantly. Beat 1 more minute after all the sugar has been added. Mixture will be a stiff, glossy meringue.

Fold in all at once: the white chocolate, nuts, liqueur, flavoring, and food coloring. Do not overstir.

Drop by large teaspoonfuls onto lined baking sheets. Place sheets in preheated oven, close the oven door, and turn off the oven. Leave cookies in oven overnight. Cookies can be stored 1 week in an airtight container; do not freeze.

VARIATION
Leave out the nuts and chocolate chips for a fat-free cookie.

Nutrition Facts Per Cookie: 48 calories, 3 g total fat (1 g saturated), 0 mg cholesterol, 6 g carbohydrate, 1 g protein, 3 mg sodium

OREGON SUNSHINE SWEETS

Orange-flavored frosting makes these extra-delicious; no one needs to know carrots make them extra-nutritious!

Yield: 48 cookies

Preheat oven to 375 degrees. Grease 2 baking sheets.

In a large bowl, combine the carrots, applesauce, shortening, sugar, egg, and vanilla. Beat well.

In another bowl, combine flour, baking powder, salt, and nuts. Add to carrot mixture, blending well.

Drop by rounded teaspoonfuls close together onto prepared pans. Bake at 375 degrees for 10 to 15 minutes.

Remove cookies from pan and cool on wire racks.

Prepare Orange Frosting by combining powdered sugar, butter, and orange peel. Add enough orange juice to reach desired consistency. Frost when cookies have cooled.

NOTE
This recipe may be doubled. Cookies freeze well for up to 3 months with waxed paper between layers. Seal cookies tightly in a box or container.

Nutrition Facts Per Cookie: 83 calories, 2 g total fat (0.6 g saturated), 5 mg cholesterol, 15 g carbohydrate, 1 g protein, 88 mg sodium

1 can (15 ounces) diced carrots, drained
½ cup applesauce
¼ cup vegetable shortening
1 cup sugar
1 large egg
1 teaspoon vanilla extract
2 cups all-purpose flour
2 teaspoons baking powder
1 teaspoon salt
½ cup finely chopped walnuts

ORANGE FROSTING
2 cups powdered sugar
2 tablespoons butter, melted
1 tablespoon grated orange peel
2–4 tablespoons orange juice

APRICOT BARS

A fancy bar cookie, equally at home at a tea or in a picnic basket.

Yield: 24 bars

Preheat oven to 350 degrees. Grease a 9x13-inch baking pan.

In a medium bowl, cream together the butter and sugar. Work in the flour and nuts. Press ¾ of the mixture in bottom of the prepared baking pan. Bake at 350 degrees for 15 minutes.

Remove from oven and spread preserves over the baked crust. Sprinkle the remaining flour mixture over the preserves. Return to oven for 20 minutes.

Cut into 24 squares while warm.

Nutrition Facts Per Bar: 281 calories, 17 g total fat (6 g saturated), 20 mg cholesterol, 33 g carbohydrate, 4 g protein, 87 mg sodium

1 cup butter, room temperature
1 cup sugar
2 cups all-purpose flour
1½ cups slivered almonds
1 cup chopped macadamia nuts
18 ounces apricot preserves

OREGON BLACKBERRY BUCKLE

½ cup butter
1½ cups sugar, divided
1 cup all-purpose flour
2 teaspoons baking powder
¾ cup milk
2½ cups fresh blackberries

Wild blackberries abound in western Oregon and this recipe makes grand use of their intense flavor.

Yield: 9 servings

Preheat oven to 350 degrees. Melt butter in an 8-inch square baking pan.

In medium bowl, mix 1 cup of sugar with the flour, baking powder, and milk. Pour into the baking pan over the melted butter.

Spread berries over the top and sprinkle with remaining ½ cup sugar.

Bake at 350 degrees for 1 hour.

Cut into 9 servings.

Nutrition Facts Per Serving: 258 calories, 6 g total fat (4 g saturated), 16 mg cholesterol, 50 g carbohydrate, 2 g protein, 143 mg sodium

THREE-BERRY PIE

1⅓ cups fresh blueberries
1⅓ cups fresh blackberries
1⅓ cups fresh raspberries
¼ cup lemon juice
¼ cup flour
½–⅔ cup sugar to taste
2 tablespoons butter
Milk

SUGARED PASTRY
2 cups all-purpose flour
½ teaspoon salt
¾ cup butter
⅓ cup ice water
½ cup sugar, divided

Enjoy the bounty of fresh berries wrapped in a sugared crust.

Yield: 8 servings

Prepare the pastry. In a medium bowl, mix together the flour and salt. Using a pastry blender or 2 knives, cut in the butter until mixture resembles coarse crumbs. Sprinkle with ice water and stir until the dough gathers together. Divide into 2 balls; wrap each in plastic wrap and refrigerate for 20 to 30 minutes.

Preheat oven to 425 degrees.

Sprinkle pastry board with ¼ cup sugar. Flatten 1 ball of dough, then roll it out, forming a circle about 12 inches in diameter. Place the dough in the bottom of a 9-inch pie pan, sugar side down.

Mix berries and lemon juice; fill the prepared pie crust with the berries. Combine flour with sugar and top the berries with the sugar mixture; dot with butter. Brush the rim of the crust with milk.

Sprinkle the pastry's remaining ¼ cup sugar on the board and roll out the second crust. Place this top crust, sugar side up, over the berries; trim and seal by crimping the edges together. Cut a few slits in the crust; brush crust with milk.

Bake at 425 degrees for 45 minutes or until golden brown. The edges of the crust may need to be covered with foil to prevent burning.

NOTE
If substituting frozen berries, thaw completely and drain before using.

Nutrition Facts Per Serving: 438 calories, 21 g total fat (12 g saturated), 54 mg cholesterol, 61 g carbohydrate, 3 g protein, 338 mg sodium

PEACH PRALINE PIE

A crunchy pecan streusel surrounds ripe peaches.

Yield: 8 servings

Preheat oven to 450 degrees.

In a medium bowl, combine peaches, sugar, tapioca, and lemon juice. Let mixture sit 15 minutes.

Meanwhile, combine the flour, brown sugar, and chopped pecans in a small bowl. Cut in the butter with pastry blender or 2 knives until crumbly. Sprinkle ⅓ of the nut mixture over the bottom of the pie crust.

Stir the peach mixture and spoon over the nut mixture in the crust. Sprinkle remaining nut mixture over the top of the filling. Garnish by using 6 pecan halves to form a star in the center of the pie. Arrange remaining 8 halves evenly spaced at crust's edge.

Bake at 450 degrees for 10 minutes. Reduce oven temperature to 350 degrees. Bake 20 minutes longer, or until peaches are tender and topping is golden brown.

Nutrition Facts Per Serving: 360 calories, 19 g total fat (6 g saturated), 15 mg cholesterol, 47 g carbohydrate, 4 g protein, 207 mg sodium

4 cups peeled and sliced peaches
½ cup sugar
2 teaspoons quick-cooking tapioca
1 teaspoon freshly squeezed lemon juice
½ cup all-purpose flour
¼ cup firmly packed brown sugar
½ cup chopped pecans
¼ cup butter
9-inch unbaked pie crust
14 pecan halves, for garnish

EGGNOG PIE

A light, festive pie to welcome the holiday season.

Yield: 8 servings

In a small bowl, soften gelatin in cold water for 5 minutes.

Meanwhile, in a double boiler, combine the egg yolks, hot water, ½ cup sugar, and salt. Cook over boiling water, stirring constantly, until the mixture coats the back of a spoon. Whisk gelatin into the custard. Cool mixture until it begins to thicken.

In a separate bowl, beat egg whites until glossy; gradually add ½ cup sugar, beating until stiff. (This amount of beaten egg whites can be microwaved on 50 percent power for 2½ minutes to kill bacteria; see Note. Cool at room temperature.) Stir in nutmeg.

Stir 3 tablespoons rum into the custard. Fold in the egg whites. Pour filling into the pie crust and chill 2 hours.

Before serving, whip cream with ¼ cup sugar and 2 tablespoons rum. Spread over the chilled filling. Sprinkle grated orange peel and chocolate over top to finish the pie.

NOTE

Eggs must sustain a temperature of 150 degrees for 3 minutes to lessen the danger of bacteria. To verify the temperature, be sure to wait 3 minutes after heating and then measure the temperature at the center of the eggs. Microwaved egg whites will not fold in as easily; overheated eggs will not fold in.

Nutrition Facts Per Serving: 341 calories, 15 g total fat (6 g saturated), 127 mg cholesterol, 43 g carbohydrate, 5 g protein, 318 mg sodium

1 tablespoon unflavored gelatin (about 1½ envelopes)
¼ cup cold water
4 large eggs, separated
½ cup hot water
1¼ cups sugar, divided
½ teaspoon salt
1 teaspoon grated nutmeg
5 tablespoons light rum, divided
9-inch baked pie crust, cooled
1 cup whipping cream, chilled
1 tablespoon grated orange peel
½ ounce unsweetened chocolate, grated

HAZELNUT CRUST
½ cup hazelnuts, roasted, skins
    rubbed off
2 tablespoons sugar
½ cup all-purpose flour
Pinch of salt
¼ cup unsalted butter, chilled, cut
    into pieces

CHOCOLATE FILLING
2 large eggs
12 ounces semisweet chocolate
    chips
2 tablespoons sugar
1 teaspoon vanilla extract
1¼ cups nonfat milk
2 tablespoons instant coffee powder
¼ cup coffee liqueur

GARNISH
Lightly sweetened whipped cream
16 whole hazelnuts, roasted
2 ounces semisweet chocolate

Chocolate Velvet Torte

This must be prepared at least six hours before serving. It's rich—it's delicious!

Yield: 16 servings

Preheat oven to 350 degrees. Grease a 9-inch springform pan.

To prepare the crust, combine nuts and sugar in a food processor with knife attachment. Process until finely ground. Add flour and salt; pulse to blend. Add butter; pulse until mixture begins to hold together. Press into bottom of the prepared pan.

Bake 20 to 25 minutes until golden. Cool on rack before filling.

In a blender, combine eggs, chocolate chips, sugar, and vanilla. Scald milk until very hot, just before boiling; immediately add coffee powder and milk to blender. Blend on low for 1 minute; let sit for 2 minutes (very hot milk heats eggs sufficiently to kill bacteria; see Note on page 119). Add liqueur and blend until smooth. Pour filling into an ungreased 9-inch square pan; chill in freezer for 1 hour.

Remove filling from freezer and stir until smooth; pour into prepared crust. Refrigerate for at least 6 hours.

Garnish torte with 20 whipped-cream rosettes. Remove skins from hazelnuts. Melt chocolate and dip nuts halfway into chocolate; place one nut in each rosette.

Nutrition Facts Per Serving: 268 calories, 17 g total fat (8 g saturated), 45 mg cholesterol, 27 g carbohydrate, 4 g protein, 25 mg sodium

1 envelope unflavored gelatin
¾ cup sugar
2 teaspoons instant coffee powder
¾ cup milk
2 large eggs, separated
¼ cup light rum
1 tablespoon sugar
1 cup whipping cream, chilled
9-inch baked pie crust, cooled
Milk chocolate curls

Coffee-Rum Pie

A subtle blending of tropical flavors.

Yield: 8 servings

In a medium saucepan, combine gelatin, ¾ cup sugar, instant coffee powder, and milk. Stir until blended. Cook over low heat 5 to 10 minutes to dissolve gelatin.

In a small bowl, beat the egg yolks. Stir half of the hot gelatin mixture into the egg yolks. Blend this mixture into the remainder of the hot gelatin in pan, stirring constantly to prevent curdling. Cook another 3 to 5 minutes.

Refrigerate mixture 20 minutes, or until it is syrupy and thick. Whisk rum into the gelatin mixture. Chill until mixture thickens again.

Meanwhile, in a large bowl, beat egg whites until stiff peaks form. Beat in 1 tablespoon sugar. (This amount of beaten egg whites can be microwaved on 50 percent power for 1½ minutes to kill bacteria; see Note on page 119. Cool at room temperature.) Fold egg whites into the chilled gelatin mixture.

Whip the cream until thick. Fold into gelatin mixture and pour into baked pie crust. Garnish with chocolate curls. Chill for 2 hours before serving.

Nutrition Facts Per Serving: 369 calories, 19 g total fat (9 g saturated), 97 mg cholesterol, 33 g carbohydrate, 14 g protein, 206 mg sodium

Chocolate Truffle Torte

Almond and chocolate exquisitely flavor the crust.

Yield: 10 servings

Preheat oven to 375 degrees.

In a medium bowl, combine flour, sugar, cocoa, and salt. Cut in butter with a pastry blender or 2 knives until the mixture resembles fine crumbs. Add almond flavoring and enough water, 1 teaspoon at a time, to bind dough. Add almonds. (This crust may also be prepared in a food processor with knife attachment.)

Press dough into bottom and up sides of 11-inch round tart pan with removable bottom. Bake at 375 degrees for 12 to 15 minutes, or until crust is set. Cool on a rack.

Meanwhile, make the filling. Melt the chocolate over low heat. In heavy, 1-quart saucepan, scald whipping cream over medium heat. Reduce heat to low and add chocolate. Stir until smooth. Pour filling into prepared crust. Refrigerate 3 to 4 hours or until firm.

Before serving, garnish by sifting cocoa over the torte. Pipe rosettes of whipped cream around border. Sprinkle chocolate shavings over whipped cream.

Nutrition Facts Per Serving: 423 calories, 30 g total fat (17 g saturated), 64 mg cholesterol, 40 g carbohydrate, 5 g protein, 75 mg sodium

CRUST
¾ cup all-purpose flour
½ cup sugar
6 tablespoons unsweetened cocoa
¼ teaspoon salt
½ cup unsalted butter, chilled
1 teaspoon almond extract
1–3 teaspoons cold water
½ cup finely chopped almonds

FILLING
10 ounces bittersweet chocolate
1½ cups whipping cream

GARNISH
1 tablespoon unsweetened cocoa
¾ cup sweetened whipped cream
Chocolate shavings or curls

Willamette Hazelnut Torte

A simple nut torte with a mocha-cream topping.

Yield: 8 servings

Preheat oven to 350 degrees. Grease an 8-inch round cake pan. Line bottom with waxed paper and grease the paper.

Sift flour and baking powder together. Set aside.

Using a food processor with knife attachment, whirl eggs and sugar until smooth. Add nuts and process until nuts are finely ground. Add flour mixture all at once and mix just until flour is incorporated. Pour into the prepared pan.

Bake at 350 degrees for 20 minutes, or until tester comes out clean.

Invert torte onto wire rack to cool. Peel off paper carefully; cool completely before finishing the torte.

For the Mocha Topping, chill a medium mixer bowl and beaters. Combine topping ingredients and whip until stiff; chill until serving time. Spread topping on cooled torte and serve immediately.

Nutrition Facts Per Serving: 292 calories, 22 g total fat (10 g saturated), 125 mg cholesterol, 21 g carbohydrate, 4 g protein, 121 mg sodium

2 tablespoons all-purpose flour
2½ teaspoons baking powder
4 large eggs
¾ cup sugar
1 cup untoasted hazelnuts

MOCHA TOPPING
2 tablespoons dry hot-chocolate mix
1 tablespoon instant coffee powder
1 pint whipping cream, chilled

CRUST
8 sheets phyllo pastry
½ cup butter, melted

FILLING
1 envelope unflavored gelatin
⅓ cup cold water
6 ounces semisweet chocolate chips
½ cup butter
1 tablespoon instant coffee powder
4 large eggs, separated
¼ cup coffee liqueur
½ cup sugar

GARNISH
1 cup sweetened whipped cream
¼ cup sliced almonds, toasted

Mocha Mousse in Phyllo

Lovely to look at, delicious to taste: a coffee lover's fantasy!

Yield: 12 servings

Preheat oven to 350 degrees. Grease a 10-inch springform pan.

Arrange 2 phyllo sheets in the prepared pan so that sheets extend up the sides. Brush lightly with melted butter. Add 2 more phyllo sheets and brush with butter. Repeat until all sheets are used. The bottom and sides of the pan should be evenly layered with pastry. Leave phyllo sheets untrimmed to make a high, elegant collar.

Bake at 350 degrees for 10 to 15 minutes; cool.

Soften gelatin in cold water in a small saucepan. Heat gently, stirring constantly, until gelatin is dissolved. Add chocolate chips, ½ cup butter, and instant coffee powder. Heat until chocolate and butter are melted; cool.

In another small saucepan, stir together the egg yolks and coffee liqueur. Cook over low heat whisking constantly until the temperature reaches 160 degrees (see Note on page 119). Mixture will be as thick as a light dough. Cool mixture.

In a large bowl set in barely simmering water, whisk egg whites with sugar until very white and foamy and the temperature reaches 160 degrees. Remove from heat; let stand for 3 minutes. Beat egg whites until stiff peaks form.

Pour ⅓ of chocolate mixture into the yolk-liqueur mixture. Whisk. Pour this mixture into remaining ⅔ of chocolate mixture. Whisk. Gently fold into egg-white mixture. Pour into cooled crust. Chill at least 2 hours.

Garnish with whipped cream and almonds.

Nutrition Facts Per Serving: 392 calories, 27 g total fat (15 g saturated), 125 mg cholesterol, 28 g carbohydrate, 11 g protein, 257 mg sodium

2 tablespoons butter, melted
½ cup milk
1 teaspoon baking powder
¼ teaspoon salt
1 cup all-purpose flour
¼ teaspoon almond extract
2 cups sugar, divided
1 can (16 ounces) pitted tart pie
    cherries, undrained
Lightly sweetened whipped cream
Almond extract to taste

Cherry Pudding-Cake

Pie cherries thrive in the Oregon climate around The Dalles on the Columbia River. This dessert, served warm with almond-flavored whipped cream, puts the cherries to good use.

Yield: 9 servings

Preheat oven to 375 degrees. Grease an 8-inch square baking dish.

In a medium bowl, stir together first 6 ingredients (butter through ¼ teaspoon almond extract) and 1 cup of sugar to make a cake batter. Pour mixture into the prepared baking dish.

In a smaller bowl, mix undrained cherries and the final cup of sugar. Pour over the batter. Bake at 375 degrees for 45 to 60 minutes.

Top with sweetened whipped cream flavored with almond extract.

Nutrition Facts Per Serving: 281 calories, 3 g total fat (2 g saturated), 9 mg cholesterol, 63 g carbohydrate, 2 g protein, 134 mg sodium

Apple Cake with Cream Cheese Frosting

An old-fashioned dessert—perfect for fall's new crop of apples.

Yield: 12 servings

Preheat oven to 350 degrees. Lightly grease a 9x13-inch baking pan.

In a large bowl, combine all cake ingredients and beat thoroughly. Pour into the prepared baking pan and bake at 350 degrees for 45 minutes. Let cake cool completely before frosting.

While the cake is cooling, prepare the frosting. In a medium bowl, cream together the butter and cream cheese until fluffy. Add salt, vanilla extract, and powdered sugar, beating until smooth. Frost cake and store in the refrigerator.

VARIATION

Instead of icing the cake with cream-cheese frosting, try serving it with Butter-Brandy Hazelnut Sauce (see below).

Nutrition Facts Per Serving: 540 calories, 24 g total fat (7 g saturated), 59 mg cholesterol, 78 g carbohydrate, 6 g protein, 293 mg sodium

2 large eggs, beaten
4 cups diced, peeled apples
2 cups sugar
½ cup vegetable oil
Dash of salt
2 teaspoons baking soda
2 teaspoons vanilla extract
2 teaspoons cinnamon
2 cups all-purpose flour
1 cup chopped pecans or walnuts

FROSTING
3 tablespoons butter, softened
6 ounces cream cheese, softened
Dash of salt
2 teaspoons vanilla extract
1½ cups sifted powdered sugar

Butter-Brandy Hazelnut Sauce

Even though this sauce stores safely in the refrigerator for several months, it's so delicious it won't last that long!

Yield: 1½ cups

In a small, heavy saucepan, combine brown sugar, syrup, butter, and salt. Cook the mixture over medium heat, stir, and with a brush dipped in cold water, wash down sugar crystals that cling to the side of the pan. When the sugar is dissolved, boil gently, undisturbed, for 12 minutes, or until a candy thermometer registers 180 degrees.

Remove pan from heat and stir in cream, vanilla extract, lime juice, brandy or whiskey, and nuts.

Pour into sterilized jars. Cover and keep refrigerated.

Serve over ice cream or cake.

Nutrition Facts Per 2 Tablespoons: 192 calories, 11 g total fat (5 g saturated), 24 mg cholesterol, 24 g carbohydrate, 1 g protein, 58 mg sodium

1 cup firmly packed light brown
    sugar
¼ cup light corn syrup
¼ cup butter
Pinch of salt
½ cup whipping cream
1½ teaspoons vanilla extract
¼ teaspoon lime juice
1½ tablespoons brandy or whiskey
½ cup coarsely chopped toasted
    hazelnuts or walnuts

¾ cup Key lime juice, divided
1 envelope unflavored gelatin
4 large eggs, separated, room
    temperature
¾ cup sugar
1 cup whipping cream, chilled
1 tablespoon freshly grated lime
    peel

GARNISH
Sweetened whipped cream
Lime slices

KEY LIME MOUSSE

Present this refreshing, light dessert in your prettiest stemmed glasses.

Yield: 6 servings

In a small bowl, soften gelatin in 2 tablespoons of the lime juice.

In a medium-sized, heavy saucepan, whisk the egg yolks with the remaining lime juice and sugar until well combined.

Cook mixture over medium heat, stirring constantly, for about 10 minutes, or until the egg mixture is slightly thickened.

Remove from heat and stir in the softened gelatin to dissolve completely. Pour mixture into a large bowl and cool to lukewarm.

In a medium bowl, beat egg whites until stiff. (This amount of beaten egg whites can be microwaved on 50 percent power for 2½ minutes to kill bacteria; see Note on page 119. Cool at room temperature.)

In a separate bowl, beat the 1 cup whipping cream until fairly stiff. Gently fold the beaten egg whites into the whipped cream. Fold this mixture into the cooled lime mixture; fold in lime peel.

Pour mousse into pretty stemmed glasses or one large glass dessert bowl; cover tightly and refrigerate about 4 hours. Mousse can be made a day ahead.

Serve garnished with sweetened whipped cream and lime slices.

NOTE
Key lime juice can be found in the bottled juice section at most grocery stores.

Nutrition Facts Per Serving: 346 calories, 18 g total fat (10 g saturated), 196 mg cholesterol, 42 g carbohydrate, 6 g protein, 94 mg sodium

6 ounces semisweet chocolate chips
2 tablespoons sugar
1 large egg
1 large egg yolk
Pinch of salt
1 teaspoon vanilla extract
¾ cup milk

POTS DE CRÈME

A five-minute recipe…too easy to ignore!

Yield: 6 servings

Place chocolate chips, sugar, egg, egg yolk, salt, and vanilla in blender.

Scald milk until very hot, just before boiling; immediately pour hot milk over ingredients in the blender. Blend 1 minute; let sit 2 minutes (very hot milk heats eggs sufficiently to kill bacteria; see Note on page 119).

Pour immediately into 6 small cups or 4-ounce dishes; chill at least 2 hours. Mixture will be thin at first but will solidify as it chills.

Nutrition Facts Per Serving: 193 calories, 11 g total fat (6 g saturated), 75 mg cholesterol, 24 g carbohydrate, 4 g protein, 30 mg sodium

Frozen White Chocolate Torte

Don't let the instructions intimidate you. Each step is easy, and the end result is a beautiful frozen dessert which can be prepared up to three days in advance.

Yield: 8 servings

To prepare crust, combine cookie crumbs and butter in a medium bowl. Press into the bottom of an 8-inch springform pan. Refrigerate crust while preparing filling.

In the top of a double boiler, melt 6 ounces chocolate, stirring often. Cool slightly.

Meanwhile, beat egg whites and cream of tartar in a large bowl until soft peaks form.

In a medium-sized, heavy saucepan, bring sugar and water to a boil, stirring until sugar dissolves. Continue boiling the syrup without stirring, until candy thermometer registers 238 degrees, soft ball stage.

Gradually beat hot syrup into beaten whites, continuing to beat until mixture is stiff and glossy and the bottom of the bowl has cooled to barely lukewarm, about 3 minutes. Fold in warm chocolate.

Refrigerate until cool but not set, about 5 minutes.

In a separate bowl, whip cream, orange liqueur, and vanilla until soft peaks form; gently fold into chocolate mixture. Fold in remaining 2 ounces chopped chocolate.

Pour filling onto the prepared crust, smoothing the top. Sprinkle with nuts. Freeze 6 hours or until firm. At this point, torte can be covered and kept frozen up to 3 days.

To prepare sauce, purée raspberries; strain to remove seeds. Stir in sugar and orange liqueur. Refrigerate until chilled, about 1 hour.

To serve torte, remove sides of pan and slice into 8 servings. Place on dessert plates and drizzle with a spoonful of raspberry sauce.

Nutrition Facts Per Serving: 557 calories, 35 g total fat (20 g saturated), 73 mg cholesterol, 59 g carbohydrate, 5 g protein, 90 mg sodium

CRUST
1½ cups macaroon crumbs
3 tablespoons unsalted butter, melted

FILLING
8 ounces white chocolate, divided and chopped
4 large egg whites
Pinch of cream of tartar
¾ cup sugar
¼ cup water
1½ cups whipping cream, chilled
1 tablespoon orange liqueur
1 teaspoon vanilla extract
3 tablespoons chopped natural pistachios

RASPBERRY SAUCE
2 cups fresh or frozen unsweetened raspberries, thawed
¼ cup sugar
2 tablespoons orange liqueur

Fromage Blanc

Serve this low-fat, frozen dessert cheese with your choice of fresh fruits, cookies, or nuts.

Yield: 6 servings

In blender or food processor, blend all ingredients, except garnish, until smooth. Pour into small ramekins or ring molds. Freeze for 2 hours.

To serve, remove ramekins from freezer and thaw until edges of the dessert melt; unmold on serving dishes. Garnish with whole fresh fruit.

Nutrition Facts Per Serving: 224 calories, 0.8 g total fat (0 g saturated), 3 mg cholesterol, 43 g carbohydrate, 13 g protein, 23 mg sodium

16 ounces nonfat cottage cheese
8 ounces low-fat sour cream
2 cups powdered sugar
2 teaspoons vanilla extract or flavoring of choice
½ cup crushed fresh fruit, optional
Whole fruit, for garnish

Gingered Pear Sorbet

4 ripe pears
½–¾ cup sugar to taste
2 tablespoons freshly squeezed
    lemon juice
1½ teaspoons finely chopped
    crystallized ginger or ⅛
    teaspoon ground ginger

GARNISH CHOICES
Mint leaves
Crystallized ginger slices or ground
    ginger
Fresh berries

So pretty served with fresh berries.

Yield: 4 servings

Peel, core, and cut pears into medium chunks.

In a blender or food processor, purée the pears with ½ cup sugar and lemon juice. Taste for sweetness, adding more sugar if desired. Add the ginger and pour mixture into an ice cube tray.

Freeze for 1 to 1½ hours or until partially frozen. Return mixture to the blender or processor and blend until smooth and fluffy but not liquid.

Pour mixture into sherbet dishes and freeze until firm, about 3 hours.

Remove sorbet from freezer and let stand at room temperature 10 to 15 minutes before serving. Garnish with mint leaves, ginger, or fresh berries.

NOTE
A quart of canned pears, well-drained, may be substituted for the fresh pears.

Nutrition Facts Per Serving: 200 calories, 0 g total fat (0 g saturated), 1 mg cholesterol, 51 g carbohydrate, 1 g protein, 0 mg sodium

Lime-Tequila Sorbet

1½ cups sugar
3 cups water
½ teaspoon grated lime peel
½ cup freshly squeezed lime juice
½ cup tequila, optional
¼ teaspoon salt

GARNISH CHOICES
Mint leaves
Lime peel curls

A light, refreshing dessert—particularly good with Mexican food. It is important to use fresh lime peel and juice.

Yield: 6 servings

In a small saucepan, stir together sugar and water; boil 5 minutes.

Add grated lime peel; boil 1 minute. Stir in lime juice and pour mixture into plastic ice cube tray. Freeze until mixture is quite thick and slushy.

Place mixture in blender; add tequila, if used, and salt. Blend to mix. Pour mixture into a freezer container and freeze.

Just before serving, stir the mixture, since it separates into layers in the freezer. Spoon into chilled individual serving dishes. Garnish with mint leaves or lime peel.

NOTE
Sorbet may be prepared in an ice-cream maker, following manufacturer's directions. The sorbet will not separate when prepared by this method.

Nutrition Facts Per Serving (with tequila): 242 calories, 0 g total fat (0 g saturated), 0 mg cholesterol, 52 g carbohydrate, 0 g protein, 93 mg sodium

GIFTS FROM THE KITCHEN

Whenever you want to say "thank you," "welcome," or "I'm glad we're friends," one of the nicest gifts you can offer is something special from your kitchen. The mixes in this section are designed for just such occasions, and depending on your packaging and presentation, they can be as plain or fancy as you wish. The mixes are also wonderful to keep on hand in your own pantry, where they can come to your rescue when unexpected company drops in, or when a jam-packed day needs a quick, easy meal.

MINESTRONE SOUP

Perfect with salad and focaccia bread!

Yield: 8 servings

10 cups water
Minestrone Soup Mix
1 pound sweet Italian sausage
3 carrots, peeled and chopped
3 stalks celery, chopped
½ cup chopped onion
1 can (28 ounces) diced tomatoes
Pasta Packet (macaroni)

Place water into a large stockpot. Add Minestrone Soup Mix and simmer for 1½ hours. If sausage is in link form, remove skin. In a medium skillet, brown the sausage, breaking it into small pieces. Add vegetables to skillet and sauté 3 to 5 minutes. Combine sausage, vegetables, and tomatoes with the soup. Bring soup to a boil and add the macaroni; simmer for 30 minutes. Add more water as needed.

Nutrition Facts Per Serving: 333 calories, 19 g total fat (7 g saturated), 43 mg cholesterol, 28 g carbohydrate, 15 g protein, 930 mg sodium

HEARTY SOUP

Keep this mix on your emergency shelf. Your family or guests will think you spent all day making homemade soup.

Yield: 8 servings

6 cups water
Hearty Soup Mix
Seasoning Packet
1 teaspoon salt
1 pound lean ground beef, browned
2 carrots, sliced
1½ cups shredded cabbage
2 cups water
15 ounces tomato sauce
24 ounces vegetable juice cocktail
Salt and pepper to taste

Put 6 cups water in a large kettle. Add Hearty Soup Mix, Seasoning Packet, and 1 teaspoon salt; bring to a boil. Cover and simmer 1½ hours. Add the remaining ingredients and simmer 20 minutes more, or until carrots are cooked. Season to taste.

Nutrition Facts Per Serving: 286 calories, 12 g total fat (5 g saturated), 43 mg cholesterol, 29 g carbohydrate, 16 g protein, 1,118 mg sodium

---

MINESTRONE SOUP MIX
¼ cup dried split peas
½ cup dried kidney beans
4 beef bouillon cubes, crumbled
2 teaspoons dried basil
1½ teaspoons dried oregano
1 tablespoon dried parsley
½ teaspoon pepper

PASTA PACKET
1 cup elbow macaroni

Gift Presentation Idea: Put the soup mix in a soup bowl; top with the macaroni in a small plastic zipper bag. Tie up with a colorful ribbon. Copy and attach preparation directions (see right).

HEARTY SOUP MIX
¼ cup split peas
⅓ cup alphabet soup pasta
¼ cup pearl barley
¼ cup lentils
2 tablespoons brown rice
½ cup dried minced onions

SEASONING PACKET
1 tablespoon dried basil
1 tablespoon dried celery flakes
½ teaspoon dried rosemary
4 teaspoons beef bouillon granules
1 tablespoon dried parsley
½ teaspoon pepper

Gift Presentation Idea: Place the soup mix in a heart-shaped container (for "hearty") with the seasoning packet in a small plastic zipper bag on top. Copy and include preparation directions (see right).

Autumn Lentils and Apricots

Great as a side dish—also as a chutney for roast lamb.

Yield: 8 side-dish servings

Autumn Lentil Mix
6 cups water
Apricot Packet
2 tablespoons vegetable oil
1 medium onion, chopped
Spice Packet
1 can (14.5 ounces) stewed tomatoes
Salt to taste
Lime juice, optional
Plain yogurt, for garnish

Place Autumn Lentil Mix and water in a large stock pot. Bring to a boil, reduce heat, and simmer for 20 minutes.

Add apricots and simmer 20 minutes more, adding more water if needed.

In a medium frying pan, sauté onion in oil. Add Spice Packet ingredients and stewed tomatoes. Cover and simmer 10 minutes.

Combine the tomato mixture with the lentil mixture; salt to taste. Simmer about 15 minutes. Remove bay leaf. If the mixture is too spicy, add a little lime juice. Top each serving with a dollop of yogurt.

Nutrition Facts Per Serving: 217 calories, 4 g total fat (0.5 g saturated), 0 mg cholesterol, 37 g carbohydrate, 12 g protein, 206 mg sodium

AUTUMN LENTIL MIX
1½ cups lentils
¼ cup dried carrots
2 tablespoons dried bell pepper
2 tablespoons dried parsley
1 teaspoon dried crushed red pepper

APRICOT PACKET
1 cup dried apricots, chopped

SPICE PACKET
1 tablespoon paprika
1 teaspoon ground cumin
¼ teaspoon ground cinnamon
1 teaspoon dried cilantro
1 bay leaf

Gift Presentation Idea: Use a pretty, airtight glass container. Place the lentils in bottom, then the dried vegetables, then a plastic zipper bag of apricots, and last, the bag of spices. Copy preparation directions (see left); tie with raffia ribbon and attach a few autumn leaves.

Herbed Couscous

Light side dish for a fish, chicken, or vegetable entrée. And so easy!

Yield: 4 servings

Herbed Couscous Mix
1½ cups water
2 tablespoons butter

Place the Herbed Couscous Mix in a medium bowl. In a small saucepan, bring water to a boil, add butter, and pour over couscous mix; stir thoroughly. Cover mixture and let rest 5 minutes. Fluff with a fork and serve immediately.

Nutrition Facts Per Serving: 309 calories, 11 g total fat (4 g saturated), 15 mg cholesterol, 46 g carbohydrate, 8 g protein, 68 mg sodium

HERBED COUSCOUS MIX
1 cup uncooked couscous
2 tablespoons dried minced onion
¼ cup raisins
¼ cup slivered blanched almonds
1 teaspoon dried oregano
1 teaspoon dried basil
1 teaspoon dried tarragon
1 teaspoon dried chives
½ teaspoon dried ground rosemary
½ teaspoon pepper

Gift Presentation Idea: Package ingredients in a brightly colored bowl—perhaps one with an African motif. Copy and include preparation directions (see left).

THREE-GRAIN PILAF MIX
⅓ cup barley
⅓ cup brown rice
⅓ cup bulgur wheat
¼ cup dried chopped onion
¼ teaspoon dried minced garlic

SEASONING PACKET
½ teaspoon salt
Dash of pepper
½ teaspoon dried oregano
¾ teaspoon dried basil

TOPPING
⅓ cup sliced almonds

Gift Presentation Idea: Package the pilaf in an interesting container—perhaps a small box decorated with shafts of wheat. Use small plastic zipper bags for seasonings and almonds. Copy and include preparation directions (see right).

THREE-GRAIN PILAF

The almond topping is a nice addition to the nutty flavor of this multi-grain dish.

Yield: 6 servings

¼ cup butter
Topping (almonds)
1 large carrot, chopped
1 cup sliced fresh mushrooms
Three-Grain Pilaf Mix
2½ cups chicken broth
¼ cup sherry
Seasoning Packet
⅓ cup chopped fresh parsley

In a large skillet, sauté the almonds in butter until toasted. Remove nuts and add carrot and mushrooms to the skillet; sauté until tender. Add Three-Grain Pilaf Mix and stir until lightly browned. Add broth, sherry, and contents of Seasoning Packet. Bring to a boil, then simmer, covered, for 45 minutes. Remove from heat and let stand 10 minutes. Toss with toasted almonds and chopped parsley.

Nutrition Facts Per Serving: 275 calories, 14 g total fat (6 g saturated), 21 mg cholesterol, 28 g carbohydrate, 10 g protein, 741 mg sodium

LEMON-DILL RICE MIX
1¼ cups uncooked long-grain rice
2 teaspoons dried grated lemon peel
2 teaspoons dried dill weed or dill seed
1 teaspoon dried minced chives
1 tablespoon chicken bouillon granules

Gift Presentation Idea: Place all ingredients in a bright yellow box and tie with a green ribbon. Add a sprig of fresh dill if available. Copy preparation directions (see right) and attach them to the ribbon.

LEMON-DILL RICE

A winning combination of flavors—perfect to accompany a fish entrée.

Yield: 6 servings

Lemon-Dill Rice Mix
3 cups water
1 tablespoon butter

In a medium saucepan, combine all ingredients; bring to a boil. Cover, reduce heat, and cook about 20 minutes, or until liquid is absorbed.

Nutrition Facts Per Serving: 124 calories, 2 g total fat (1 g saturated), 5 mg cholesterol, 26 g carbohydrate, 1 g protein, 477 mg sodium

Gingerbread Hotcakes

Especially tasty when served with whipped cream and pineapple or coconut syrup.

Yield: 12 hotcakes

½ cup melted butter
1¼ cup medium-dark molasses
1 large egg, beaten
Gingerbread Hotcake Mix
¾ cup black coffee, cold

Using an electric mixer, combine first 3 ingredients in a bowl until well blended. Add the Hotcake Mix alternately with the cold coffee; blend thoroughly.

Preheat griddle to a slightly lower temperature than for regular pancakes; grease griddle. Drop batter from a ¼-cup measure; cook until bubbles form on the top and the underside is brown. Turn and brown the other side.

NOTE
To make waffles with the mix, separate the egg, blending the yolk with the molasses and butter. Whip the egg white until firm but not stiff and fold in after other ingredients have been combined.

Nutrition Facts Per Hotcake: 247 calories, 8 g total fat (5 g saturated), 38 mg cholesterol, 41 g carbohydrate, 2 g protein, 330 mg sodium

GINGERBREAD
HOTCAKE MIX
2½ cups all-purpose flour
1½ teaspoons baking soda
1 teaspoon ground cinnamon
1 teaspoon ground ginger
½ teaspoon ground cloves
½ teaspoon salt

Gift Presentation Idea: Package mixed ingredients in a plastic zipper bag, then a brown paper bag decorated with stenciled gingerbread boys or girls. Copy preparation directions (see left) and use a red ribbon to attach directions and to tie up the bag.

Poppy Seed Pancakes

A healthful, multigrain pancake, crunchy with poppy seeds.

Yield: 12 to 15 pancakes

Poppy Seed Pancake Mix
2 large eggs, beaten (or ½ cup egg substitute)
3 tablespoons oil
1¾ cups buttermilk

In a medium bowl, combine the Pancake Mix with the rest of the ingredients. Beat just until smooth; do not overbeat.

Drop batter from a ¼-cup measure onto a hot, greased griddle; cook until bubbles form on the top and the underside is brown. Turn and brown on the other side.

Nutrition Facts Per Pancake: 142 calories, 6 g total fat (1 g saturated), 37 mg cholesterol, 17 g carbohydrate, 6 g protein, 162 mg sodium

POPPY SEED
PANCAKE MIX
¾ cup whole wheat flour
½ cup soy flour
¾ cup all-purpose flour
2 teaspoons baking powder
½ teaspoon baking soda
1 tablespoon sugar
3 tablespoons oat bran
2 tablespoons poppy seeds

Gift Presentation Idea: Package mixed ingredients in a plastic zipper bag, then place in a white paper bag. Tie bag with red paper poppies. Copy and attach preparation directions (see left).

FOCACCIA BREAD

Top this Italian flatbread with pesto for an accompaniment to soup. Toppings of cinnamon and sugar, or ricotta cheese and canned sour cherries turn this bread into dessert.

Yield: 6 servings

Focaccia Bread Mix
1½ teaspoons dried rosemary (omit if making a sweet dessert focaccia)
½ cup warm water (110–115 degrees)
4 tablespoons olive oil, divided
Salt

Place Focaccia Bread Mix and dried rosemary in a large glass mixing bowl. Add the warm water and 2 tablespoons of the olive oil.

Blend the dough with a wooden spoon until smooth. If it seems dry, add a bit more water; if it seems sticky, add a bit more flour.

Turn bread onto a floured board and knead until smooth. Transfer to an oiled bowl; rotate dough to coat the surface with oil. Cover bowl with plastic wrap and let rise in a warm spot until dough is doubled in bulk, about 1 hour.

Preheat oven to 425 degrees. On a floured board, punch down dough and roll into the desired shape—a round, a rectangle, or small individual rounds. Place shaped dough on an oiled baking sheet and brush with the remaining 2 tablespoons oil. Sprinkle with salt.

Bake 5 minutes; then with a fork, pierce air bubbles on the surface. Continue baking 8 minutes longer or until golden brown. Remove from baking sheet and add toppings, if desired.

Nutrition Facts Per Serving: 218 calories, 10 g total fat (1 g saturated), 0 mg cholesterol, 28 g carbohydrate, 5 g protein, 180 mg sodium

FOCACCIA BREAD MIX

1 package active dry yeast
1 tablespoon sugar
1½ cups bread flour
½ teaspoon salt

Gift Presentation Idea: Mix all ingredients in a large plastic zipper bag. Tie it up in a red-and-white checkered napkin. Copy preparation directions (see right) and tuck in along with a wooden mixing spoon.

DILLY BEER BREAD

Quick, easy, and so good. And a wonderful aroma to greet family or guests.

Yield: 8 servings

Dilly Beer Bread Mix
1 can (12 ounces) beer

Preheat oven to 350 degrees.

In a medium bowl of an electric mixer, combine Dilly Beer Bread Mix and beer. Beat for 3 minutes, scraping beaters after 2 minutes. Put batter into greased 9x5-inch loaf pan; smooth top. Bake at 350 degrees for 40 to 45 minutes.

Remove bread from the pan and place on a wire rack to cool. Best served warm.

Nutrition Facts Per Serving: 205 calories, 0.5 g total fat (0.1 g saturated), 0 mg cholesterol, 42 g carbohydrate, 5 g protein, 598 mg sodium

DILLY BEER BREAD MIX

3 cups self-rising flour
3 tablespoons sugar
1 tablespoon dried dill weed
1 tablespoon dill seed
2 tablespoons dried minced onion

Gift Presentation Idea: Mix ingredients in a large plastic zipper bag; place bag alongside a can of beer in a loaf pan. Tie up with a colorful ribbon. Copy and include preparation directions (see right).

AGGIE BREAD

Imagine, homemade bread and no preparation dishes to wash!

Yield: 4 servings

Baggie Bread Mix
⅓ cup warm water (90–100 degrees)

Open the Bread Mix bag and pour in the warm water.

Zip bag closed and squish and squeeze until all the flour disappears and dough is very smooth. This is the "kneading."

Let the dough rise in the bag in a warm place until the dough appears to have doubled in size.

Open the bag and turn out the dough onto a floured surface. Knead 10 to 15 times. Shape dough into a loaf and place in a greased 6x3x2-inch bread pan.

Let the bread rise again until the loaf is double in size, about 45 minutes.

Bake at 375 degrees for 20 to 25 minutes or until golden brown.

Remove bread from the pan and place on a wire rack to cool.

Nutrition Facts Per Serving: 120 calories, 0.4 g total fat (0 g saturated), 0 mg cholesterol, 25 g carbohydrate, 4 g protein, 268 mg sodium

BAGGIE BREAD MIX
1 cup all-purpose flour
1 teaspoon sugar
1 teaspoon active dry yeast
½ teaspoon salt

Gift Presentation Idea: Combine ingredients in a gallon-sized plastic zipper bag. Close the bag and work it until the ingredients appear to be mixed. Place the bagged mix in a 6x3x2-inch bread pan and wrap it in a colorful fabric bag. Copy and enclose preparation directions (see left).

NOTE
This is a perfect gift for a child who is learning to cook.

ARDAMOM-CURRANT SCONES

An emergency-shelf staple—makes a wonderful breakfast treat for unexpected guests.

Yield: 18 scones

Cardamom-Currant Scone Mix
½ cup butter, cut into small pieces
1 large egg, beaten
½ tablespoon freshly squeezed lemon juice
½ cup sour cream

Preheat oven to 400 degrees. In a medium bowl, combine all ingredients. Turn out onto a floured board and knead briefly.

Gently roll out dough to ½-inch thickness. Cut into 2-inch rounds and place on greased baking sheet. Bake at 400 degrees for 10 minutes.

Nutrition Facts Per Scone: 125 calories, 7 g total fat (4 g saturated), 28 mg cholesterol, 14 g carbohydrate, 2 g protein, 126 mg sodium

CARDAMOM-CURRANT
SCONE MIX
2 cups all-purpose flour
¾ teaspoon baking soda
1½ teaspoons cream of tartar
⅛ teaspoon salt
1 teaspoon ground cardamom
½ cup currants

Gift Presentation Idea: Thoroughly mix dry ingredients, stir in currants, and package in an attractive airtight container. Put container in handled basket with a selection of teas and jams. Copy and include preparation directions (see left). Top with a 2-inch round biscuit or cookie cutter.

 GLÖGG

In Sweden, this is called Christmas Wine, but it's wonderful on any cold night.

Yield: 6 servings

1 bottle (750 ml) dry red wine
1½ cups water
Glögg Mix
GARNISH
2 tablespoons raisins
1 tablespoon sliced almonds

In a large saucepan, combine red wine, water, and Glögg Mix. Over medium heat, bring mixture slowly to the boiling point. Strain and serve hot, garnishing each serving with raisins and almonds.

Nutrition Facts Per Serving: 242 calories, 1 g total fat (0.2 g saturated), 0 mg cholesterol, 40 g carbohydrate, 2 g protein, 15 mg sodium

 HOT MULLED CIDER

This fruitful blend fills the kitchen with a mouth-watering aroma. Having several of these spice bags on hand makes it easy to brew up a potful of cider on any cold winter day.

Yield: 8 servings

Hot Mulled Cider Mix
4 cups apple cider
2 cups water
2 cups orange juice
¼ cup lemon juice

Heat all ingredients to boiling point. Remove from heat, then let stand a few hours to blend flavors. Before serving, reheat and strain. Serve in mugs.

Nutrition Facts Per Serving: 145 calories, 2 g total fat (0.4 g saturated), 0 mg cholesterol, 36 g carbohydrate, 1 g protein, 21 mg sodium

---

GLÖGG MIX
¾ cup raisins
1 tablespoon whole cardamom
1 tablespoon whole cloves
2 sticks cinnamon, broken into pieces
½ cup sugar

Gift Presentation Idea: Package ingredients in a plastic zipper bag and place in a colorful, seasonal stein. Copy preparation directions (see right) and attach them to the stein handle with a colorful ribbon. Accompany with a bottle of wine.

HOT MULLED CIDER MIX
¼ cup sugar
6 whole cloves
2 cinnamon sticks
4 whole allspice

Gift Presentation Idea: Package seasoning mix in a small plastic zipper bag and place it in a mug. Copy preparation directions (see right) and tie them to a cinnamon stick poked into the mug. Add a bottle of cider, if desired.

Basic Salsa

Accompanied by tortilla chips, salsa is becoming an American favorite!

Yield: 6 servings

Basic Salsa Mix
1 can (14.5 ounces) diced tomatoes or 16 ounces diced fresh tomatoes
2 ounces canned diced green chilies, optional
Chopped jalapeño chili pepper to taste, optional

Add Basic Salsa Mix to diced tomatoes. For hotter salsa, add chilies to taste. Crush mixture to desired consistency. Refrigerate salsa after mixing.

Nutrition Facts Per Serving: 23 calories, 0.3 g total fat (0 g saturated), 0 mg cholesterol, 5 g carbohydrate, 1 g protein, 294 mg sodium

Sweet Hot Mustard

A good all-purpose spread for sandwiches or smoked meats.

Yield: 3 cups

Sweet Hot Mustard Mix
1 cup cider vinegar
3 large eggs, slightly beaten

Mix together Mustard Mix and vinegar, whisking to combine. Cover and refrigerate overnight. The next day, in a 2-quart saucepan, add the beaten eggs to the mustard mixture. Cook over medium heat, stirring constantly, until mixture thickens to pudding-like consistency. Pour mixture into sterile jars. Refrigerate for up to ten days or freeze for up to two months.

Nutrition Facts Per Tablespoon: 32 calories, 1 g total fat (0.1 g saturated), 13 mg cholesterol, 5 g carbohydrate, 1 g protein, 4 mg sodium

Oregon is particularly important to Christmas. The state leads the nation in the production of Christmas trees and English holly, and this holiday bounty decorates homes across the nation.

GREEK HERB
SEASONING MIX

1½ cups dried parsley
¼ cup dried minced onion
¼ cup dried minced garlic
¼ cup dried oregano
¼ cup dried minced chives
3 tablespoons dried basil
2 tablespoons dried dill weed
2 tablespoons dried mint
1 tablespoon dried rosemary
1 tablespoon pepper
1½ tablespoons dried lemon peel
1 teaspoon ground cinnamon
1 tablespoon dried fennel seed

Gift Presentation Idea: Mix ingredients together thoroughly. Package in 7 or 8 spice jars decorated with braid or ribbon with a Greek design. Copy and attach suggested uses (see right).

BOUQUET GARNI MIX

½ cup dried thyme
½ cup dried bay leaves
½ cup dried rubbed sage
½ cup dried rosemary
32 rectangles (4x8 inches each)
    cheesecloth
Butcher's string

Combine crumbled herbs. Fold cheesecloth to make squares; place 1 tablespoon of mix in the center of each. Gather edges and tie with string, leaving a generous end of string to attach a fresh sprig of parsley when the packet is used.

Gift Presentation Idea: Place several packets in an attractive tin. Copy and include useful information (see right).

GREEK HERB SEASONING

A versatile seasoning with many uses. Try our suggestions or create your own!

GREEK-STYLE FISH
Sprinkle herb mix lightly over fillets of fresh, firm white fish, such as ling cod or true cod. Drizzle with olive oil and bake at 375 degrees until fish flakes easily with a fork.

GRILLED GREEK CHICKEN
Rub chicken pieces with herbs and lemon juice; refrigerate 1 to 3 hours before grilling or broiling.

POT ROAST
Rub roast with herbs, add water, and bake according to your favorite recipe.

SOUPS AND STEWS
Add this seasoning mix to taste to enhance the flavor of many soups and stews.

SUMMER SQUASH
Sauté zucchini and other summer squash. Add a squirt of lemon juice and a dash of herb seasoning.

GREEK DIP
Combine 1 tablespoon herb mix with 8 ounces of plain yogurt; chill 1 to 2 hours to blend flavors. Serve with fresh vegetables or toasted pita bread triangles.

BOUQUET GARNI

These little packets of herbs are more convenient to use than reaching for several spice jars.

USEFUL INFORMATION
Garni is a traditional French seasoning used to flavor soups or stews. Tie a few fresh sprigs of parsley to a garni before it goes in the soup pot. Remove packet of herbs before serving.

Feel free to experiment by adding other herbs to the basic ones already in this garni.

ℬING CHERRY CHUTNEY

Outstanding with meats or over cream cheese as an appetizer.

Yield: 12 to 14 half-pint jars

In a large pan, bring vinegar and sugars to a boil, dissolving sugar. Add remaining ingredients and return to a boil. Reduce heat and simmer for one hour or until thick.

Wash jars and keep hot until needed. Prepare lids as manufacturer directs.

Ladle hot chutney into one hot jar at a time, leaving ¼-inch head space. Wipe jar rim with a clean damp cloth. Attach lid. Fill and close remaining jars.

Process half-pints in a boiling water bath for 10 minutes (15 minutes 1,000 to 3,000 feet; 20 minutes above 3,000 feet).

Nutrition Facts Per ¼ Cup: 62 calories, 0.3 g total fat (0 g saturated), 1 mg cholesterol, 15 g carbohydrate, 0 g protein, 83 mg sodium

¾ cup cider vinegar
1 cup firmly packed brown sugar
1½ cups sugar
8 cups dark sweet cherries, pitted and halved
½ cup diced onions
1 cup raisins
2 cloves garlic, minced
2 teaspoons mustard seed
3 tablespoons chopped crystallized ginger
2 teaspoons salt
½ teaspoon cayenne pepper

Gift Presentation Idea: Wrap the jar in cellophane, gathering it on top of the jar; hold in place with wire twist while you add the final ribbon touch.

𝒫EACH-GINGER CHUTNEY

An exotic accompaniment to curries, or any chicken, lamb, or duck dish.

Yield: 14 half-pint jars

The day before canning, peel and cube the peaches into ½-inch pieces. Cover with a brine of the salt and 2 quarts water. Cover and let stand in a cool place for 24 hours.

When ready to cook the chutney, peel and slice the ginger root into very thin slices. Cover slices with water in a saucepan and bring to a boil; reduce heat and simmer 50 minutes or until slices are tender. Drain ginger, reserving ½ cup of the ginger water.

In a large, nonaluminum saucepan, mix reserved ginger water, sugar, vinegar, and garlic; bring to a boil. Drain the peaches and add them to the saucepan; cook slowly until peaches are transparent. Remove peaches from the syrup and set aside.

To the syrup, add cooked ginger, onions, lime juice, ground ginger, dried chili pepper, and raisins. Cook over medium-low heat until thick, about 1½ to 2 hours, stirring occasionally.

While the mixture is cooking, wash jars and keep hot until ready to fill. Have canning kettle filled with hot water for processing. Prepare lids as manufacturer directs.

When chutney has thickened, return peaches to the mixture and cook 5 minutes.

Ladle mixture into prepared jars, one at a time, leaving ¼-inch head space. Wipe jar rim with a clean damp cloth; attach lid. Fill and close remaining jars. Process half-pints in a boiling water bath for 10 minutes (15 minutes 1,000 to 3,000 feet; 20 minutes above 3,000 feet).

NOTE
Unprocessed chutney may be stored in the refrigerator for a short time or frozen.

Nutrition Facts Per ¼ Cup: 147 calories, 0.1 g total fat (0 g saturated), 0 mg cholesterol, 38 g carbohydrate, 1 g protein, 32 mg sodium

8 pounds peaches (about 24)
¼ cup plain salt (without iodine)
1 pound fresh ginger root
½ cup ginger water (see directions)
7 cups sugar
3 cups cider vinegar
4 large cloves garlic, chopped
2 cups chopped onion
1½ cups lime juice
1½ teaspoons ground ginger
1 dried red chili pepper, crushed
1 cup golden raisins
1 cup seedless raisins

Gift Presentation Idea: Cross-stitch a peach on a 4-inch circle of fabric. Gently remove the jar ring from finished jar of chutney; center the peach design and screw the ring back in place. For a nice effect, add a tuft of fiberfill or cotton under the fabric.

Medley of Flavored Vinegars

Herb vinegars are playing an increasingly important part in lighter eating trends. They are a simple way to add zest to salads, sauces, and marinades. A homemade gift of a flavored vinegar is easy to prepare—simply gather together a pretty bottle, a sprig of herbs or some berries, and some vinegar.

Individual taste and availability of products will determine what you use in making flavored vinegars. You can use one herb or a combination; it's fun to experiment. Decide which flavor you want dominant and adjust the amounts of each herb accordingly. Here are some suggestions to help you get started.

Rosemary and tarragon
Garlic and chives
Basil and mint
Dill and chives
Basil and blueberries
Mint
Nasturtium leaves
Violets
Lavender
Roses
Raspberries
Strawberries
Blackberries

Gift Presentation Idea: Simply add a ribbon to the bottle and attach a tag identifying the type of vinegar.

Fresh herbs or fruits are a must! If you have a garden, harvest herbs and fruits in the morning; wash and dry your bounty.

The best vinegar choices for making most flavored vinegars are white wine, champagne, and Japanese rice vinegars.

Bruise the herbs or fruit slightly (a wooden spoon works well) before placing them into a clear glass bottle or jar. For a pint of vinegar, use one of the following: 1 cup of herb leaves, ¼ cup grated herb root, 1 to 2 tablespoons herb seeds, 1 cup herb flowers, 4 cloves garlic, or 1 cup berries.

Use one of these 2 methods: *Either*, pour the vinegar over the crushed herbs and close container tightly with a nonmetallic lid. Set the container in a warm place out of direct sunlight for 2 to 3 weeks. Shake the container once every other day. After 2 to 3 weeks, taste the vinegar, and if it is not flavored enough, let it stand longer until it reaches the flavor you desire. *Or*, heat the vinegar to the simmering point and pour it into the container holding the crushed herbs. Close tightly with a nonmetallic lid. Keep the jar at room temperature. Start testing the vinegar in a few days to determine when the flavor is just right.

When the vinegar flavor suits you, pour the vinegar through a nonmetallic strainer into a glass jar or pitcher. Then filter it 2 to 3 times, using either cheesecloth or coffee filters. Be sure you end up with a clear product.

Use a nonmetallic funnel to pour the strained vinegar into the final bottle; add a fresh sprig or flower of the herb or berries to the bottle. Seal bottle and store in a cool, dark place. A flavored vinegar should be used within a year.

The Douglas Fir, Oregon's state tree, is known for its great strength, stiffness, and moderate weight. Reputed to be "stronger than concrete," Douglas Fir lumber is an integral component of buildings worldwide.

ACKNOWLEDGMENTS

PATRONS

The generosity of the following companies and individuals is greatly appreciated:

ASSISTANCE LEAGUE OF CORVALLIS MEMBERS

KEITH A. DRAGOO & ADRIENNE BURGER DRAGOO

DOROTHY & JOHN FENNER

GOOD SAMARITAN HOSPITAL

HENNESSY FAMILY

MCHENRY FUNERAL HOME, INC.

STARKER FORESTS, INC.

TOWN & COUNTRY REALTY

WASTE CONTROL SYSTEMS, INC.

COOKBOOK COMMITTEE

Chairman
Linda T. Dunn

Assistant Chairman
Barbara McMinds

Editor
Linda J. Ahlers

Computer Production
Verlyne Phillips

Production Coordinator
Anita Cook

Recipe Editor
Shirley "Sam" Olsen

Food Editors
Frankie Botts
Gene Newburgh

Section Chairman
Elaine Sutherland

Appetizers
Adrienne Dragoo
Barbara Mullins

Soups
Pat Eckhout
Virginia Hunt

Salads
Jane Bohman
Carol Laub

Breads and Brunch
Virginia Garthwait
Elsa McCloskey

Entrées
Mary Jane Grieve
Alberta Peterson

Side Dishes
Carole Boersma
Beverly Johnson

Desserts
Ann Hilderbrand
Marc Kemper

Gifts from the Kitchen
Pat Coolican
Sally Walker

Ingredients Editor
Eleanor Wight

Index Editor
Corey Arentz

Researchers
Ginny Adams
Corey Arentz
Carole Beedlow
Henny Chambers

Treasurer
Diane Lorenz

Pine cone illustration by Allen Q. Wong

CONTRIBUTORS

Assistance League of Corvallis thanks all its members, families, and friends who were instrumental in bringing *Beautiful, Bountiful Oregon* to publication. If we have omitted any name from our list inadvertently, we offer our sincere regrets.

Adams, Ginny
Ahlers, Linda
Ansell, Audrey
Ansell, Melody
Arentz, Corey
Ball, Jane
Barratt, Dorotha
Becker, Joyce
Beedlow, Carole
Birdsall, Betty
Bjarnsen, Vicki McCallie
Black, Barbara
Blair, Pat
Boersma, Carole
Bohman, Jane
Bonander, Delores
Bonham, Christine
Botts, Frankie
Bracken, Wendi
Brandis, Kathryn
Brehm, Bunny
Buck, Beth
Buck, Jane
Burt, Beryl
Caldwell, Doris
Calvin, Shirley
Carter, June
Chambers, Henny
Chandler, Jean
Christensen, Marilee
Church, Addie
Church, David
Clement, Lin
Cook, Anita
Coolican, Pat
Coolican, Stephen
Coolican, Susan
Copeland, Ann
Cowger, Donna
Cracraft, Kay
Cumming, Ruth
Cummings, Margaret
Dane, Louise
Dawson, Kay

Downing, Betty Lou
Dragoo, Adrienne Burger
Dragoo, Carol
Dunn, Linda
Eckhout, Pat
Edwards, Barbara George
Elder, Millie
Elliott, Colleen
Entrikin, Lynne
Fenner, Dorothy H.
Flood, Mary Anne
Freilich, Shoshannah
Garthwait, Virginia
Gleason, Carol
Goodmonson, Sharon
Gray, Kim
Green, Valerie
Grieve, Mary Jane
Griffin, Pat
Hamilton, Brenda
Hansen, Lia
Harger, Virginia
Harris, Kay
Hatch, Emily Gilchrist
Hauge, Claire
Hector, Ada T.
Hector, Cynthia
Heilig, Marcia
Heimbigner, Margaret
Henderson, Alice
Henderson, Fred
Henry, Ruth
Hirsch, Fred
Hirsch, Judy
Hilderbrand, Ann
Howard, Mary
Hunt, Virginia
Jackson, Christa
Jackson, Susan Wight
Jenks, Pat
Johnson, Ann
Johnson, Beverly
Joiner, Marje
Jorgensen, Cisco
Kahlbaum, Maka
Kane, Denise
Kelsey, Mary
Kemper, Marc
Kimura, Kiko
Kobriger, Kathleen
Lathen, Becky
Laub, Carol
LeChevallier, Mary
Leeland, Lucille
Leklem, Darlene
Lewis, Karen
Levy, Anne
Linderman, Lynne
Llewellyn, Linda Bianchi

Lords, Beverly
Lorenz, Diane
Loucks, Marge
Ludwig, Margie
Marks, Barbara
Martin, Amy
May, Bob
McCloskey, Elsa
McCumber, Judith
McKeehan, Nina
McKinnon, Julie Kennedy
McLean, Georgia
McLean, Marilyn
McMinds, Barbara
Mellen, Kim
Mendoza, Patti McCallie
Merickel, Marlea
Merten, Diane
Miller, Beth
Mondich, Carol
Monilaws, Catherine
Monteith, Betty
Mosciallo, Anna
Moss, Patsy
Mueller, Karen
Mueller, Maria
Mullins, Barbara
Musch, Connie
Nagy, Sherrie
Nakashima, Miriam
Nearing, Frances
Neufeld, Mrs. Herman
Newburgh, Gene Compton
Newburgh, Marilyn
Newburgh, Tate
Neville, Lynne
Nordhausen, Lynn
Norris, Betty
Oehler, Nellie
Oettinger, Elizabeth
Oja-Munson, Nancy
Olsen, Shirley "Sam"
Orloff, Carole
Palmer, Mardee
Parker, Joellen
Peters, Deanna
Petersen, Jean
Peterson, Alberta
Peterson, Shirley
Phillips, Verlyne
Poole, Susan
Popovich, Jeanne
Powell, Sandy
Reistad, Kathleen

Reynolds, Cherie
Riley, Bea
Ringo, Jane
Roberts-Dominguez, Jan
Rodriguez, Juanita
Rosendahl, Jean
Sarff, Marilyn
Schreck, Jacque
Schudel, Dianne
Schudel, Linda
Schudel, Paula
Seeds, Eleanor
Selsor, Roberta
Settles, Sue
Seyb, Helen
Slatt, Mabel
Slaughter, Marcia
Smith, Joyce
Smith, Nita
Smith, Renee
Soenksen, Elfriede
Sowle, Irene
Sparrow, Alice
St. Clair, Kim
St. Clair, Marian
Stebbins, Monine
Stephens, Evelyn
Stephenson, Genny
Stewart Layton, Karla
Stewart, Gladys
Stockwell, Deanna
Strandberg, Becky
Straughan, Pat
Sutherland, Charles
Sutherland, Elaine
Tarrant, Jean
Thomas, Margie
Thompson, Kim
Truax, Nancy
Vars, Freda
Verdugo, Loretta Satariano
Verdugo, Louis
Vomocil, Sally
Walker, Sally
Wasiczko, Karen
Webber, Hazel
Wedman, Rachel
White, Barbara
Whitesell, Gwen
Whitman, Linda
Wight, Eleanor
Wilcox, Margaret
Williams, Carol H.
Williams, Donna
Williams, Marci
Witt, Ellen
Wohlwend, Pat
Wong, Gloria
Wood, Kathryn
Younger, Patty

INDEX